THESE WORDS UPON THY HEART

*"And these words, which I command thee
this day, shall be upon thy heart; and thou
shalt teach them diligently unto thy children . . . "—Deuteronomy 6:6, 7.*

These Words Upon Thy Heart

SCRIPTURE AND THE CHRISTIAN RESPONSE

BY

HOWARD TILLMAN KUIST

*Charles T. Haley Professor of Biblical Theology for the
Teaching of English Bible
in Princeton Theological Seminary
Princeton, New Jersey*

1947

John Knox Press

RICHMOND, VIRGINIA

To my family

THE JAMES SPRUNT LECTURES

Mr. James Sprunt, of Wilmington, North Carolina, in 1911 established a perpetual lectureship at Union Theological Seminary in Virginia, which would enable this institution to secure from time to time the services of distinguished ministers and authoritative scholars as special lecturers on subjects connected with various departments of Christian thought and Christian work. The lecturers are chosen by the Faculty of the Seminary and a Committee of the Board of Trustees, and the lectures are published after their delivery in accordance with a contract between the lecturer and these representatives of the institution.

The series of lectures on this foundation for the year 1946 is presented in this volume.

B. R. Lacy, Jr., *President*

Union Theological Seminary
in Virginia

FOREWORD

THE INVITATION of the Faculty and Trustees of Union Theological Seminary in Virginia to deliver the Sprunt Lectures for the year 1946 came as a most unexpected expression of confidence and generosity. It had been my privilege to have a part in the training of seven different Union Seminary classes between the years 1938 and 1943. The opportunity to return to the campus in Ginter Park to renew and deepen the ties formed during those years of teaching was one which I deeply appreciated.

The present volume consists of the six lectures, substantially as delivered between February 25 and March 2, 1946, in Schauffler Hall. By permission of the publishers, chapter one appeared as an article in *Theology Today* for July, 1946. The purpose, scope, and plan of the series is outlined in the Introduction. In the Appendix beginning at page 159 there is an abridgment of Ruskin's *Essay on Composition,* which will assist materially in the reading of chapter three. The brief introductory note on page 160 discusses the significance of this essay.

As these lectures now go to a wider audience I should like through them to greet many more of my former students, and to re-enkindle the warmth of our previous associations at The Biblical Seminary in New York, Gettysburg Lutheran Seminary, Union Theological Seminary in Virginia, The General Assembly's Training School, and more recently at Princeton Theological Seminary. I am greatly indebted to a number of friends, and particularly to Dr. Donald G. Miller, of Union Theological Seminary, Richmond; to Miss Mary Virginia Robinson, of the John Knox Press; and to my wife, Leone Marquis Kuist, for valuable suggestions in preparing the manuscript for publication.

HOWARD TILLMAN KUIST.

CONTENTS

༄

INTRODUCTION

"With St. Paul there is a responsible center of manhood where all decisive acts are done. Given in terms of mental science this practical notion would, perhaps, amount to this: The heart is man's inherent capacity for free, personal decision. By the heart therefore individual thoughts and feelings are converted into intention."—Olin A. Curtis.

These Words Upon Thy Heart

&

INTRODUCTION

AT A LOW MOMENT during the world depression in the 1930's one of
our most competent historians, Mr. James Truslow Adams, analyzed
the world situation in terms of a threefold crisis: an economic crisis,
a political crisis, and what he called "a crisis in character." He proceeded to prove that the third was by far the most grave and far-
reaching. Turning to our own country he concluded: "If there is
to be a regeneration of the national character it can come about only
by the regeneration of each of us as individuals. It is not a matter of
committees, machinery, and organization. It can come only from
some subtle change in the heart of the individual American man and
woman."[1]

Mr. Adams did not indicate how this "subtle change" was to be
brought about. As an historian all he did was to underscore its imperative necessity. How to initiate and to order vital control in human relations is no new problem. It is as old as the human race.
But whether old or new it is charged today with mortal urgency.
Now it is a matter of life or of death. World history will not wait
indefinitely for decision. How will mankind respond to this gravely
accentuated crisis in character? Two words employed by Mr. Adams,
and used apparently with deliberation, indicate the kind of response
required.

The first is the word *individual*. Individual men and women, he
says, are the key to this crisis. One of the causes of the mounting
chaos and bewilderment in our human world today is the disappear-

ance of the individual in the mass. In economic relations the individual is lost in the corporation and the union. In political movements the individual citizen disappears in the party, the state, and the United Nations. In military life he is lost in a uniform. How to restore personal responsibility; how to disentangle the individual from the mass; how to recover a due sense of the importance, the dignity, and the worth of the individual man and woman is at the root of the world problem. The British historian Arnold J. Toynbee, in the Burge Memorial Lecture for 1940, concurs in this view when he declares that, "The spiritual progress of individual souls in this life will in fact bring with it more social progress than could be attained in any other way." And he supports his view by adding: "It is a paradoxical but profoundly true and important principle of life that the most likely way to reach a goal is to be aiming not at that goal itself but at some more ambitious goal beyond it. This is the meaning . . . of the saying in the New Testament about losing one's life and saving it."[2] If world events of the past decade have taught any one lesson it is this: that world order and security must never depend upon a few great men. But the influence of many common men, fused by common loyalties and good will, can remake the world. If humanity survives its present ordeal it would be safe to say that our times will be recorded in the annals of history not as the Atomic Age, but as the Age of the Common Man.

The second significant word employed by Mr. Adams is the word *heart*. The subtle change to which he refers must be wrought out, according to his view, in the heart. The word heart is one of our most commonly employed metaphors. A metaphor, as one of our Semantic experts suggests, can never be regarded merely as embroidery—"embroidery which improves the appearance of our linen but adds nothing to its utility."[3] Mr. Adams, the historian, is hardly indulging in embroidery when he speaks of the heart. What utility has this word heart in defining the world problem? Without any doubt heart has found its way into our popular speech through the influence of the Bible, for it is one of the most characteristic words of its vocabulary. In its broadest sense the word heart (the Hebrew *lēb*) is used in the Old Testament to refer to the many-sided expressions of man's moral character. Any general reader of the Bible is familiar with such expressions as a clean heart; a contrite heart; an understanding heart; a wise heart; or a glad heart.[4] He also recalls such expressions as a proud heart; an evil heart; a revolting heart; a deceitful heart; a haughty heart; etc.[5] But this expression of man's moral character denoted by the word heart is still more sharply defined by specific references to the various activities of personal life, as for example: the thoughts of the heart; the desires of the heart; the imagination of the heart; and the devices of the heart.[6] In other words, by the use of this word *lēb* the Old Testament recognizes a variety of activities in a man's inner life which influence the formation of his character. Sometimes the whole inner life of a man appears to be gathered together in one single impulse, as in the words of the Psalmist: "With my whole heart I have sought thee: O let me not wander from thy commandments."[7] Jesus and Paul who inherited the Old Testament view of man's nature used the Greek *kardia* (heart) in much the same way.[8] It is clear from these examples that the Bible uses the word *heart* to refer to man's inherent capacity for self-determination, as influenced by his thoughts, his affections, his imagination, or his will. The highest exercise of this capacity is realized when a man by conscious personal intention enthrones God as the Lord of his life.

Mr. Adams and the Bible are in agreement that the world problem is essentially the heart problem. But Holy Scripture gives a lucid and urgent commentary upon the undefined "subtle change" for which Mr. Adams calls. Two basic yearnings of the common man exhibit themselves in every age and in every nation. They are the yearning for length of days and the yearning for fullness of life in the good land. Moses and the prophets in the Old Testament, Jesus and the apostles in the New, insisted that these yearnings could neither be satisfied nor realized apart from the enthronement of God in the common life.

Jesus offered a comprehensive summary of the Law in His words quoted from two Old Testament passages: "Hear, O Israel; The Lord our God, the Lord is one: and thou shalt love the Lord thy God with all thy heart, and with all thy soul, and with all thy mind, and with all thy strength," and "thou shalt love thy neighbor as thyself."[9] These are old words indeed, but pregnant today with new meaning. The solution of the heart problem, according to the Scriptures, involves the fulfillment of these relationships for which no other experience can ever be an effective substitute. So crucial did Moses recognize the fulfillment of these relationships to be that he urged: "These words, which I command thee this day, shall be upon thy heart; and thou shalt teach them diligently unto thy children, and shalt talk of them when thou sittest in thy house, and when thou walkest by the way, and when thou liest down, and when thou risest up."[10] *These words . . . upon thy heart!*

The prophets of Israel recognized two particular obstacles to the enthronement of divine truth in human relations. The first of these was preoccupation. The prophets observed the tendency of their contemporaries to walk "after things that do not profit,"[11] or to spend their money for that which is not bread, and their labor for that which satisfieth not.[12] They made it their vocation to challenge this preoccupation by forceful and repeated proclamation of the claims of God: "Incline your ear, and come unto me; hear, and your soul shall live."[13] A second obstacle, the concomitant of the first, the prophets pronounced to be insensitivity. "Seeing, they see not," said Jesus,[14] while Isaiah, sensing the approaching doom of his people, declared: "The harp and the lute, the tabret and the pipe, and wine, are in their feasts; but they regard not the work of Jehovah, neither have they considered the operation of his hands. Therefore my people are gone into captivity for lack of knowledge."[15]

The only salt which can save modern society from further disintegration is increased knowledge of God and His ways. And the best instrument for challenging man's preoccupation with purely mundane affairs and for awakening his awareness to the "operation of

God's hands" is Holy Scripture. The subject for the present series of Sprunt Lectures is *These Words Upon Thy Heart*. This title has been chosen to emphasize and to illustrate the instrumental worth of Holy Scripture in forming responsible Christian character. Our first task will be to indicate how Scripture is qualified to do this by examining the nature of its appeal to the common man. Chapter one therefore will deal with this subject. Our second task will be to explore the method of response Scripture requires. We propose to examine and to illustrate the elements of procedure recognized as basic in the study of the humanities, and to indicate how they may be embodied effectively in understanding Scripture. Chapters two, three, and four will be devoted to this exposition. We will conclude the series with two chapters in which the adequacy of such a method of apprehending Scripture will be related to man's freedom to think and to his motives for action.

NOTES

The quotation on the title page of the Introduction is from Olin A. Curtis, *Personal Submission to Jesus Christ,* p. 12.

1. James Truslow Adams, "The Crisis in Character" in *Harper's Magazine,* Vol. 167, August 1933, pp. 257-267.
2. Arnold J. Toynbee, *Christianity and Civilization,* Burge Memorial Lecture for 1940, p. 41. London, Student Christian Movement.
3. S. I. Hayakawa, *Language in Action,* p. 192. N. Y. Harcourt, Brace and Co., 1941.
4. See Psalm 51:10,17; I Kings 3:9; Proverbs 8:5; 11:29; 15:13.
5. See Proverbs 16:5; 21:4; Jeremiah 3:17; 5:23; 17:9; Proverbs 18:12.
6. See Psalm 33:11; Jeremiah 23:20; Psalm 37:4; I Chronicles 29:18; Proverbs 6:18.
7. Psalm 119:10, 34, 58, 69, 145.
8. E.g. Mark 2:8; 7:21; 12:30; Romans 6:17; I Corinthians 4:5; II Corinthians 9:7.
9. Mark 12:29-31. See Deuteronomy 6:4, 5; Leviticus 19:18. Permission to quote from the American Standard Version of the Revised Bible (copyrighted by the International Council of Religious Education) is hereby gratefully acknowledged.
10. Deuteronomy 6:6, 7.
11. Jeremiah 2:8.
12. Isaiah 55:2.
13. Isaiah 55:3.
14. Matthew 13:13.
15. Isaiah 5:12, 13.

SCRIPTURE AND THE COMMON MAN

"*Holy Scripture is the history of men in a constitution; a history of men not seeking relations with God, but men having such relations, and whose task is now to believe in these relations, and to maintain them.*"
—*Richard C. Trench.*

"*To discover the Common Man is, of course, to discover that which all men have in common . . . Knowledge of God and knowledge of the Common Man are closely akin. Some think them identical.*"—*L. P. Jacks.*

ONE

Scripture and the Common Man

ह&

SIR EDWIN LANDSEER once painted a picture of a fire burning in a domestic grate. The fire glowed with so strange and marvelous a radiance that when the painting was exhibited in the Royal Academy in London scores of visitors came from near and far to behold the miracle. Eventually the artist sold the painting for a handsome price. After a few years, however, the purchaser had to summon the artist. "Please come and relight your fire," he urged; "it has gone out." Landseer now realized that he had used a very brilliant but fugitive pigment and so the glow of his fire had faded.[1]

The fate of Landseer's painting is a parable of the all too common mortality among the works of man. The material ingredients of a work may limit the measure of its greatness. Other works, however, have an incandescence maintained by a secret source. This is true of the writings preserved for us in the Bible. Their ingredients, although made out of the stuff of common life, nevertheless are pervaded by a spirit whose flame is as deathless as the needs of men. They are like the fire which Bunyan's Christian beheld in the Interpreter's House, where the deeper meaning of his pilgrimage was symbolically unfolded to him. "Then I saw in my dream," says Bunyan, "that the Interpreter took Christian by the hand, and led him into a place where was a fire burning against a wall, and one standing by it, always casting much water upon it, to quench it; yet did the fire burn higher and hotter." When Christian inquired the meaning of this strange sight, he was led to a place behind the wall, "where he saw a man with a vessel of oil in his hand, of the which he did also continually cast (but secretly) into the fire."[2]

Bunyan's allegory, which pictures the hidden secret of Christian experience and the way in which "the work of grace is maintained in the soul," is also an eloquent symbol of the vitality of Christian Scripture. For the flame of Christian truth and life is one. At the flame of Scripture humble men and women for hundreds of generations have found the fire with which to kindle their sacrifices. And so the word of truth in Scripture has become the deed of truth in Christian experience. Most of us could offer illustrations of this fact out of our own personal experience or that of our friends. Such was the experience of Augustine St. Clare, who in speaking of his mother to his cousin, said: "The Bible was my *mother's* Book. By it she lived and died . . . Why, Cousin, that mother has been all that has stood between me and utter unbelief for years. She was a direct embodiment and personification of the New Testament, a living fact to be accounted for, and to be accounted for in no other way than by its truth."[3] Humble men and women like this mother are the light of the world. The glow of divine truth in their hearts makes them stand like shining lamps, despite their

> ". . . weight of cares
> Upon the great world's altar-stairs
> That slope through darkness up to God."[4]

But how, we may well ask, does the word of truth in Scripture enkindle and maintain this spiritual glow?

THE MEANING OF THE WORD SCRIPTURE

Our English word Scripture, derived from the Latin *scriptura*, carries a twofold significance which has direct value in elaborating our theme. In the first place, the Latin *scriptura* (from the Latin *scribo*, "I write") referred originally to anything written: a line, written characters or signs, an inscription, a writing, or a book. Illustrations of its use are quite abundant in Latin literature. G.

Velleius Paterculus[5] uses it to refer to an inscription; Martial[6] to a transcript; Suetonius[7] to a brief note; Cicero[8] to a written composition; Tacitus[9] to an official paper of the state. In its native Latin associations, any sign, symbol, or writing which served as a medium of communication was *scriptura,* scripture. But the word came to enjoy its most distinguished use when employed to translate the Greek *graphē,* or the plural *graphai,* as applied first to the Old Testament, then to the New, and finally to the whole Bible. The Vulgate, for instance, uses the word *scripturae* to translate the Greek *graphai* when referring to prophetic writings in the Hebrew Bible, as in Matthew 26:56, where Jesus is speaking to His captors in the garden of Gethsemane. He says, "This is come to pass, that the scriptures of the prophets might be fulfilled." Augustine used it in relation to the New Testament, when in his *Confessions* he referred to these "apostolic" writings as being the Holy Scriptures.[10] The Old and New Testaments which comprise our Bible came in time to be known as Holy Scripture. These writings were set apart from all other sacred documents and from all secular associations as embodying what Christians recognized to be the revealed will of God. Our English word scripture, then, has a twofold implication derived from the Latin *scriptura:* the one, a universal reference to any writing or form of communication; the other, a distinctive reference to divine truth enshrined in the Bible. There are likewise two ways in which Scripture may be viewed.

THE TWO SIDES OF SCRIPTURE

Holy Scripture has two sides. On the one side it is like all other writings, both sacred and secular. Like the side of the wall which Bunyan's Pilgrim approached in the Interpreter's House, a side which was open to the view of all comers, Scripture may be studied as are all other writings. On this side Holy Scripture is presented to men in the familiar forms of literature, as history or poetry, proverb or parable, discourse, meditation, or apocalypse. In this sense Scripture, regarded as a medium of communication, has a close affinity to all the arts. The essence of language, as Otto Jespersen has said, is "human activity—activity on the part of one individual to make himself understood by another, and activity on the part of that other to understand what was in the mind of the first."[11] Viewed simply as a vehicle of communication, Scripture calls for the same mutuality of understanding, the same immediacy of experience, and the same self-activity which men ordinarily give to any writing.

But while the Scriptures are like all other writings they have another side on which they are distinctly different. And until they are seen to be different, the reader is like the Pilgrim in the Interpreter's House who has not yet seen the other side of the wall. He may be attracted by the glow but he does not understand the secret of its radiance. In the moments of deep need when the comman man yearns for freedom from life's entanglements, when he seeks light for his darkness, food for his heart's hunger, and quenching for his soul's thirst, he turns to Scripture, but not for its charm as literature, nor for its artistic excellence, nor even for its contribution to his knowledge of history, or of law, or of social theory. He turns to Scripture for what it can do to lift him out of his earth-bound experience into the pure light of God. Here every man may behold not only the true image of himself as a human being, but also the true shape of his own destiny: what by the grace of God in Christ he may become.

It lies beyond the scope of the present study to explore the theological problem involved in defining the nature of Scripture as revelation. During the past two decades many valuable contributions to the literature on this subject have been made. The names of John Baillie, Karl Barth, Nicholas Berdyaev, Emil Brunner, E. P. Dickie, Karl Heim, Edwin Lewis, John Mackay, H. R. Mackintosh, and Nathan Söderblom are but indicative of the widespread and mounting interest in the subject of revelation.[12] Our concern in the present study is not to be with the nature of revelation, but with the kind of response revelation requires. E. P. Dickie, in the Kerr Lectures for 1937 entitled *Revelation and Response,* stated the matter clearly in his suggestion that "revelation and response go hand in hand."[13] Where human response is lacking, the revealing process cannot be complete. It is written into the very constitution of man, and experience offers many lucid illustrations of the fact, that in his quest for spiritual illumination, ere a man can find what he seeks, he must first be prepared to give. W. Cosby Bell put the whole matter correctly when he affirmed that "in all reflection a point is always reached where, before further progress can be made, something must be done." The Christian faith "is neither a system of thought alone, nor yet just a program of action, but a spirit of enterprise in which thought and action shall co-operate."[14] We may therefore appropriately consider two aspects of Scripture which indicate its distinctive fitness to win an effective response in personal experience. First, the adequacy of Scripture as a center of illumination. Second, the adequacy of the appeal in Scripture to motive.

THE ADEQUACY OF SCRIPTURE AS A CENTER OF ILLUMINATION

In his search for satisfying spiritual illumination, it is a true instinct which leads the common man to look for an authoritative word from a level which is higher than that which the plane of secular literature can provide. No one has stated this better than Lawrence Hyde in his *Prospects of Humanism*:

"It is not going too far to suggest that every individual who pursues his search for spiritual illumination with a sufficient persistence finally finds himself obliged to leave secular literature behind him. The divine as it is glimpsed from a distance by the earth-bound giant is not enough for him. He must sit at the feet of those who, even if they are less sympathetic figures, owe their authority to the fact that they are standing on more elevated ground. He must study *scripture*, a type of utterance which comes from a center different from that from which the corrupted mortal is speaking . . . The sacred is not to be confounded with the secular word. It is not as-

piring upwards, but bringing the light downwards to earth . . . It is
written by men . . . who have turned their backs on the world . . .
And it expounds a wisdom which is not of this world . . . It is only
by looking upwards that man can obtain light."[15]

It is to be carefully observed that Mr. Hyde is not speaking here
of Holy Scripture. He is merely distinguishing between secular and
sacred literature. He is not arguing in support of divine revelation.
He believes that the religion of the churches is a dead religion.[16]
He has no sympathy with existing religious organizations of a traditional type. But he *does* recognize the plight of the common man
in his yearning for spiritual illumination. He also correctly discerns
that the same man follows a perfectly right instinct when he seeks
such illumination on a level higher than that of secular literature.
Furthermore, he detects, although through a glass darkly, the true
incandescent light of Holy Scripture. Speaking of the so-called
"emancipated" men who find no glow in sacred literature, he declares, "They will read Dostoevsky with avidity—chiefly because he
lived a large part of his time in Hell, with the topography of which
they themselves are perfectly familiar. But they forget that Dostoevsky himself was a passionate student of the New Testament."[17]

Here Mr. Hyde detects what makes Holy Scripture different.
Dostoevsky did write letters from the abysmal depths of the under-
world. But he had stood also upon the heights where the light of
Scripture had burst upon his soul and where he had eaten of its
bread. Where, for instance, did he get his finely drawn ethical sense
expressed in the words which he puts into the mouth of the newly
converted Markel, "Everyone is really responsible to all men for all
men and for everything"?[18] Nor need we ask why he has the Russian
monk, in his reference to those who seek to rule by intellect alone,
without Christ, say, "They aim at justice, but denying Christ they
will end by flooding the earth with blood."[19] The New Testament
had left its mark on Dostoevsky as it does on every other mortal who
finds in it a type of utterance which "brings light downwards to
earth" from a center totally different from that from which the cor-

rupted mortal is speaking. The Holy Scriptures qualify as the supreme book of mankind by virtue of their distinctive fitness to awaken, to invigorate, and to mold the spiritual life of man with genuine Christian character. This fitness was used by Richard C. Trench as an argument for their divine inspiration. Drawing his evidence from widely different aspects of human experience he concluded, "Good men and holy men, and the best and wisest of mankind, the kingly spirits of history enthroned in the hearts of mighty nations, have borne witness to its influences, have declared it to be beyond compare the most perfect instrument, the only adequate organ, of humanity; the organ and instrument of all the gifts, powers, and tendencies by which the individual is privileged to rise above himself . . . in order to find his true self . . . in the ever-living Word."[20]

THE ADEQUACY OF THE APPEAL IN SCRIPTURE TO MOTIVE

The fitness of Scripture as an organ of cultivating the spiritual life of man is seen in its appeal to motive. James G. K. McClure, writing of the origin and influence of the Bible among English-speaking people, traces the evidence of its creative power in education, its formative influence over literature, its vitalizing force in the missionary enterprise, and its effects upon the general life of the English-speaking world. He concludes that "the vital principle of the Bible is not its code but its motive . . . Its rules of behavior may be found here and there in other religions, philosophies, and teachings, but not its motive. The message of the Bible is that man comes to his glory only in self-sacrificing and helpful love."[21] Scripture is much more than a source book of doctrine or ethics. It is a summons to action. Scripture insists that a man will never really come to know God in whose image he has been created, by whom in Christ he has been redeemed, and for whom he has been made, until he first makes up his mind about himself. At its core Scripture has something which must be reckoned with by conscious deliberate action. In its appeal to a supernatural power that alone can energize the entire person, Scripture shows how the center of gravity in personal life must be shifted from self to God and how this shift is to be effected. This special note in its appeal must engage the activities of the whole man.

Every man is faced by the peril of rationalizing his quest for spiritual illumination. In other words, when confronted by a choice he is tempted to make it upon a level which will be at the least possible cost to himself, or in line with his own chosen self-interest. This decisive aspect of personal experience, so potent for good or ill, is what Prof. Olin A. Curtis has described as the blockade of motive. "Why is it not necessary," he asks, "for a person to will the thing in which at the moment he has the greatest interest?" He answers, "Because in the protective action of personality under pressure there is a complete blockade of motive . . . until the individual can look his motives over to choose and use any motive he has. He cannot create motive, he cannot act without motive, but he can select any motive high or low, weak or strong, which lies within his range of constant interest. The motive does not seize the man, but the man seizes the motive."[22] This of course does not mean that a person always scrutinizes his consciousness when making a decision. Most acts in practical experience rise spontaneously from life, and sometimes it is difficult, if not impossible, for an individual to know from what motive he is acting. However, it is possible when once a person *has* acted to observe where his interest actually lies and thus to recognize the stuff of which he is made. Furthermore, when a person by the light of Holy Scripture is thus enabled "to read the fine print of his own soul,"[23] that is, to become conscious of the right motive, or the highest motive, he never acts without an inward knowledge of right or wrong. The Psalmist understood this when he asserted:

"I have refrained my feet from every evil way,
That I might observe thy word."[24]

And the author of the Fourth Gospel recognized this power of divine truth to unfold the motives of an individual's acts to himself, when he observed:

"And this is the judgment, that the light is come into the world, and men loved the darkness rather than the light for their works were evil. For everyone that doeth evil hateth the light, and cometh not to the light, lest his works should be reproved. But he that doeth the truth cometh to the light, that his works may be made manifest, that they have been wrought in God."[25]

In opening a way for every man to "do truth" by selecting true and vital motives of action, Holy Scripture calls for a corresponding response of Christian manhood. In winning this response from the individual it leaves him a different person, a person marked by the grace of Christian character.

THE FRUITFUL BY-PRODUCTS OF SCRIPTURE

This adequacy of Scripture as an instrument of spiritual illumination and as an effective power of unfolding motive is indicated further by its fruitful by-products in human experience. For no sooner does an individual discover new light, or experience deeper insights into its divine truth, than he spontaneously desires to give expression to it in word or deed. And so the Bible has come to be woven into the broad fabric of human experience and world history by inspiring and nurturing the creative spirit of man. George Eliot declared, for instance: "I studied the Bible every day until the end so as to learn the analysis of the motives that determine men, and to learn also the progress of sin when once it gets into the soul."[26] The Bible has thus mothered those arts which conserve and advance its eternal truth in Christian story, in poetry and song, in Christian painting and architecture, in Christian symbolism and literature. This profound creative impulse is accompanied by a corresponding peril. Strangely enough, men have a tendency to become so preoccupied with these fruitful by-products that they lose vital touch with the creative fount itself. Without realizing it they become accustomed to the half-light of secondhand perceptions and depend more and more upon some recognized expert to elucidate its truth for them. As a result, rival systems of interpretation compete with each other to win adherents from those who have had no firsthand experience with the records themselves. This readiness to accept secondhand benefits of spiritual culture is but one among many evidences of the secularizing spirit of modern life, and it is against this that one of our competent critics has protested. "For," says he, "with the steadily increasing secularization of our thought since the beginning of the modern scientific age we have come to accept more and more completely the assumption that the qualifications for elucidating truth in every sphere of enquiry are almost purely intellectual . . . The only people who have any legitimate claim to deal with these matters are those who have familiarized themselves with the vast technical literature, who conduct their discussions in an unintelligible jargon, whose mental processes are all but incomprehensible to the man in the street."[27] While we may be profoundly thankful for every benefit which has come from specialized learning, this tendency to refer major concerns to the specialist has created the popular impression that spiritual understanding is beyond the range of the ordinary person. This in turn has induced a sense of frustration, a feeling that nothing much can be done about it. At the same time man's spiritual hunger goes unsatisfied, and as a consequence, great masses of people fall easy prey to cults and sects which pretend to offer spiritual food. We may, therefore, profitably turn our attention to still another aspect of our subject by considering the relation of the common man to the expert.

THE COMMON MAN AND THE EXPERT

Two characteristics of man in his quest for illumination on life may now be considered. The first of these is the desire for a sure footing. Even as a child he exhibits this trait when he asks, "How tall is that building?" The question does not betray any want of perception on his part. What he wants to know is that his perceptions are reliable so that he may walk with confidence. Does he actually see what his eyes tell him is there? This yearning for inner assurance, made evident in his questions about the nature of the outer world, is even more urgent in relation to his own inner experience. In theological language this is what is called the craving for authority. When it comes to those matters which involve the springs of his inner being, a man wants to hear a clear, sure voice which tells him he is right and so sets his heart at peace and his mind at rest.

But this craving for authority is accompanied by a second trait of human nature, a bent to evade responsibility for his own acts. Ibsen has ably illustrated this in his character Peer Gynt. When viewing his own private way of life, Peer Gynt declares:

> "The essence of the art of daring,
> The art of bravery in fact
> Is this: To stand with choice free foot
> Amid the treacherous snares of life.
> To know for sure that other days
> Remain beyond the days of battle.
> To know that ever in the rear
> A bridge for your retreat stands open.
> This theory has borne me on,
> Has given my whole career its color."[28]

Both of these characteristic human traits, the yearning for a higher wisdom and the bent to evade responsibility, are reflected in the Genesis account of the Garden of Eden. When the woman saw "that the tree was to be desired to make one wise, she took of the fruit thereof, and did eat; and she gave also unto her husband with her, and he did eat." But when confronted by God's question, "Hast thou eaten of the tree?" the man said, "The woman whom thou gavest to be with me, she gave me of the tree, and I did eat." And the Lord God said unto the woman, "What is this thou hast done?" And the woman said, "The serpent beguiled me, and I did eat."[29]

This bent to escape responsibility, united with the craving for authority, drives the common man to seek the aid of the expert—someone who is competent; someone who knows; someone who can and will represent him at the court of his own conscience. "The natural man," as Rudolph Sohm has correctly observed, "is a born Catholic. From these impulses of the natural man, born at once of his longing for the Gospel and his despair of attaining to it, Catholicism has arisen. Herein lies the secret of the enormous power it has over the masses."[30]

The common man with his deep sense of personal need exhibits these same characteristics when he turns to Scripture for spiritual illumination. It is true that in Scripture he expects to hear the mighty and transforming voice of the living God. Yet secretly he would like to have his own perceptions of its truth confirmed; or at least he would prefer to have some recognized expert tell him, this means *this,* or that means *that.* Recognizing these traits which make the natural man a born Catholic, the Reformers emphasized the necessity and the obligation of private judgment. By asserting this principle, they did not mean to suggest that any man has the privilege of finding whatsoever he will in Scripture (as their views are sometimes falsely interpreted). But they were counseling against this perverse human tendency to shift responsibility to someone else. Every man before God is responsible finally for himself. This is the very essence of Reformed Christendom.[31] What the Scriptures proclaim *publicly*—that is, their universal truth, open to the view of every individual who possesses the requisite sensitivity to their message—every man must make his own *private* concern; this he must make his own personal possession. And the reason is obvious. The word of faith by which the Christian lives is not any external authority but an inward grace. The Apostle Paul, who coined the expression "word of faith," uses it in connection with a passage from the book of Deuteronomy, part of which he quotes in his Epistle to the Romans:

"For this commandment which I command thee this day, it is not too hard for thee, neither is it far off. It is not in heaven, that thou shouldst say, Who shall go up for us to heaven, and bring it unto us, and make us to hear it, that we may do it? Neither is it beyond the sea, that thou shouldst say, Who shall go over the sea for us, and bring it unto us, and make us to hear it, that we may do it? But the word is very nigh unto thee, in thy mouth, and in thy heart, that thou mayest do it."[32]

Deep in personality there is a region where no external aid however valuable can assist the individual and where he, and he alone, must act if his response to truth is to be normal. This normal mode of spiritual understanding, combined with Christian action, is essentially one of sight and not wholly one of reason. Here a man must depend not upon explanations offered by someone equipped with special knowledge, but upon his own inherent powers. This is not to say that the specialist cannot offer valuable assistance. He can offer information which involves matters beyond the range of ordinary knowledge, like historical data. He may make accessible contributions available only in a foreign language. He can explain what is obscure, and give evidence for his claims, though of course he can do so only to the extent to which he has explored. But he cannot endow another individual with the gift of sight. This is the gift of the Creator alone, which every man must cherish and must cultivate by actual use. Every man must see for himself or he does not see at all. Whoever has this gift of sight in any measure can improve his sight by self-discipline. He can correct his sight by repeatedly opening it to the light. Honesty of vision, and the improvement of imaginative insight, constitute for every man, both expert and the man of the street, what John Oman has happily described as both "a discipline and a duty."[33]

Holy Scripture, therefore, makes certain imperative claims upon both expert and common man alike. The accomplishments of the expert give him obvious advantages over the layman. But his special qualifications to inquire into truth carry with them the obligation to use them in advancement from the point where every man stands before God on the same level. Before the light of Holy Scripture, specialist and common man alike share the privileges and obligations of all mortal men. First, the privilege of confidence and freedom in the pure light of God's self-disclosures in Scripture to men. The corresponding obligation consists in loving God with heart and mind and soul. Second, the privilege of self-knowledge coming from these luminous disclosures of Scripture in his own inner life and experience. The corresponding obligation is the exercise of his personal integrity in word and deed. Third, the privilege of belonging in Christ to the redeemed humanity from the bosom of which Scripture speaks. This is accompanied by the obligation of community—the loving of one's neighbor as one's self.

Thrown back ultimately upon himself both by privilege and by obligation, it follows that the quality of an individual's response to Scripture will depend both upon the exercise of his capacity to understand and upon the extent to which he seriously commits himself to the fulfillment of his obligation as a Christian.

THE COMMON MAN AND HIMSELF

If the claims of Christian faith upon a response of the whole man constitute the distinctive note of Scripture, then whatever will bestir a man to a livelier, fuller, and more mature exercise of this capacity to understand will be advantageous toward securing the response of his entire manhood. The present effort in liberal education to develop the full values which the humanities offer to the common life therefore has a relation also to the use of Holy Scripture. For the disciplines which are cultivated by humanistic studies concern themselves with "the apprehension, analysis and interpretation of expressed insights in the realms of morality, religion, art and literature."[34]

No one will deny the sad inability of the average person today to clarify his own thinking or to express himself with precision, due partly at least to the failure of the schools to give adequate training in these basic disciplines. Recent extended studies made at the adult level "show that from one-third to two-fifths of the adult population of the United States are unable to read with ease and understanding material of sixth grade difficulty."[35] This deficiency in general literacy without any doubt is at least partially responsible for the widespread spiritual illiteracy of our day. One task to which the prophets of Israel gave themselves was to open blind eyes and to unstop deaf ears that they might perceive the privileges and obligations of revealed truth.[36] A return to the humanities in education will be a distinct aid toward restoring this prophetic spirit to higher education and to serious study of the Bible in particular.

In 1940 two contributions of major importance in this field were published. Neither of these contributions at the time, nor since, has received the attention it deserved, due to the exigencies of global war. The time has now come to recognize the primary value of these contributions with special reference to their significance for the use of Scripture. The two volumes to which we refer are *The Arts and the Art of Criticism,* by Theodore Meyer Greene, and *The Humanities,* by Louise Dudley and Austin Faricy.

The Arts and the Art of Criticism is the product of collaboration between Professor Greene and specialists in six major arts over a period of years. It is addressed to serious students and critics of the several arts as well as to reflective laymen. The book is primarily philosophical in character, and is the only work in this field which approaches definitive proportions. Three specific contributions of this work which have a bearing on the use of Scripture may be mentioned. First, ample demonstration is made of the fundamental kinship between the several arts as well as of their essential differences. The six major arts used to illustrate these likenesses and differences are music, the dance, and architecture as typical of the abstract arts; sculpture and painting which illustrate the representative arts; and literature as an example of symbolic art. Even a cursory glance at the synopsis printed on a single sheet at the end of the volume reveals that, viewed in terms of composition, all the arts are one. By reproducing and analyzing nearly three hundred specific examples Professor Greene avoids the pitfalls of generalization and sets forth concretely the distinctive characteristics of the major arts. Thus he enables the individual to draw upon his own powers of appreciation to view a work of art as "an object of delight, a vehicle of communication, and, at least potentially, a record of significant insight."[37] In the book no direct application of these principles is made to their use in the appreciation of Scripture, but their synoptic relevance is obvious.

A second contribution is Professor Greene's formulation of critical standards applicable to all the arts by defining and illustrating three essential aspects of every work of art. These basic categories of artistic analysis which assist the individual to explore a work systematically are matter, form, and content. It is here that Professor Greene's work has an immediate and positive relation to Biblical studies, although he has not deliberately stated it. Since the Bible as a medium of communication exists in a literary form, it comes within the orbit of the arts and therefore these same essential categories of artistic analysis apply with equal validity to the apprehension of expressed insights in Holy Scripture. When once this affinity between Scripture and the arts is recognized, a new day dawns in the life of any person who contemplates or enters upon serious study or teaching of the Bible.

A third primary contribution of *The Arts and the Art of Criticism* is the distinction drawn between three aspects of criticism: historical, re-creative, and judicial. By showing their mutual interdependence as a part of one organic process as well as the distinctive function of each in the arts, Professor Greene has indirectly rendered a distinct service to Biblical studies where clarification between these aspects of criticism is sorely needed, and where a reorientation of the whole field, to bring historical and re-creative processes into a more adequate balance, is urgently required. The average layman is both confused and irritated by the way in which specialists talk down to him and make the Bible a jumble of historical and critical problems. Upon the other hand there is no surer way of conserving and advancing the invaluable contributions of modern historical study than by practicing the principles of re-creative method which Professor Greene has so clearly defined and illustrated.

The Humanities is a less philosophical and a more practical treatment of the same disciplines discussed by Professor Greene. It also is the result of collaboration. Over a period of twelve years at Stephens College, in Columbia, Missouri, an experimental course was conducted for the purpose of integrating the study of the arts and at the same time "to focus attention on an understanding and appreciation of the individual masterpiece."[38] The class grew in twelve years from a single section of only fifteen students to twenty-five sections, enrolling over six hundred students. This book is the product of their guided experimentation in this field, emphasizing a threefold approach. The arts are considered in the light of their common principles. The vocabulary and equipment are supplied by which any individual can make his own criticism and analysis, and realize his own appreciation. And the specific work of art is used directly without recourse to any other medium. The relation between these procedures and firsthand appreciation of Scripture is obvious. For the same capacities which men commonly exercise in opening the eyes of their understanding to nature and to the arts should render them correspondingly sensitive to the essential appeal of Scripture.

Here, then, is a "sound of marching in the tops of the mulberry-trees" which may well lead all Bible lovers to bestir themselves.[39] The arts and Scripture are alike in their appeal to immediacy of impression. Holy Scripture is unique in the imperative claims it makes upon the individual to realize full-grown Christian manhood. Divine revelation requires the response of the whole man. The same disciplines which sharpen his eye and ear to promote artistic discernment and to increase his capacity for aesthetic delight are open avenues to his intelligent use of Holy Scriptures. Every correct response becomes under God the vestibule of a more intimate revelation of His Being. Like the Chambered Nautilus which leaves "the past year's dwelling for the new," the individual, upheld by God's free Spirit, finds himself in a more stately mansion of Christian character, until at last he is set free to leave his "outgrown shell by life's unresting sea."[40]

NOTES

The quotations on the title page of this chapter are found in R. C. Trench, *Hulsean Lectures for 1845*, pp. 28, 29; and L. P. Jacks, *The Confession of an Octogenarian*, pp. 151, 152. The Macmillan Company, New York, 1942.

1. As reported by Jan Gordon, *The London Observer*, April 1, 1934, p. 5.
2. John Bunyan, *The Pilgrim's Progress*, Part I. Section on the Interpreter's House.
3. See Harriet Beecher Stowe, *Uncle Tom's Cabin*, pp. 180 and 218. People's Library, 52.
4. Tennyson, *"In Memoriam,"* lv.
5. G. Velleius Paterculus, *History of Rome*, 2, 61, 3.
6. Martial, *Epigrams*, 1, 66, 3.
7. Suetonius, *The Deified Julius*, 41, 9.
8. Cicero, *Concerning Oratory*, 1, 33, 150.
9. Tacitus, *Annals*, 3, 3, 5.
10. Augustine, *Confessions*, Book III, (V), 9, where "scripturas sanctas" refers back [see III, (IV), 8] to his quotation of Col. 2:8, 9, and his reference to such writings as "apostolica."
11. Otto Jespersen, *The Philosophy of Grammar*, p. 17. London, Allen and Unwin, 1924. Jespersen continues, "These two individuals, the producer and the recipient of language, or as we may conveniently call them, the speaker and the hearer, and their relations to one another, should never be lost sight of if we want to understand the nature of language." See also Jespersen: *Mankind, Nation, and Individual from a Linguistic Point of View*, p. 4, Harvard University Press, 1928; and T. C. Pollock, *The Nature of Literature*, pp. 12-20, Princeton University Press, 1942.
12. The literature on this subject is most extensive. The following recent works in English are representative: John Baillie and Hugh Martin, editors, *Revelation*, A Symposium, by Gustaf Aulén, Karl Barth, Sergius Bulgakoff, M. C. D'Arcy, T. S. Eliot, Walter M. Horton, William Temple, Macmillan, New York, 1937. Karl Barth, *Church Dogmatics*, Vol. I, *The Doctrine of the Word of God*, T. & T. Clark, Edinburgh, 1936. Nicholas Berdyaev, *Freedom and the Spirit*, Scribners, New York, 1935. Emil Brunner, *The Mediator*, Lutterworth Press, London, 1934, and *The Divine-Human Encounter*, Westminster Press, Philadelphia, 1943. E. P. Dickie, *Revelation and Response*, T. & T. Clark, 1938. Karl Heim, *God Transcendent*, Nisbet, London, 1935. Edwin Lewis, *A Philosophy of the Christian Revelation*, Harpers, New York, 1940. John A. Mackay, *A Preface to Christian Theology*, Macmillan, 1941. H. R. Mackintosh, *The Christian Apprehension of God*, The Student Christian Movement Press, London, 1929. Nathan Söderblom, *The Nature of Revelation*, Oxford University Press, New York, 1933.
13. E. P. Dickie, *Revelation and Response*, p. 253.
14. W. Cosby Bell, *Sharing in Creation*, pp. 11, 12. Macmillan, New York, 1925.
15. Lawrence Hyde, *The Prospects of Humanism*, pp. 162, 163. Scribners, New York, 1931.
16. *Ibid.*, p. 168.
17. *Ibid.*, p. 163.

18. Dostoevsky, *The Brothers Karamazov*, p. 356. The Modern Library, New York.
19. *Ibid.*, p. 394.
20. Richard C. Trench, *The Fitness of Holy Scripture for Unfolding the Spiritual Life of Man:* The Hulsean Lectures for 1845, pp. 17, 18. Second Edition, revised. Macmillan, Cambridge, 1847.
21. James G. K. McClure, *The Supreme Book of Mankind,* The Origin and Influence of the English Bible, The Bross Lectures, 1929, p. 216. Scribners, New York, 1930.
22. Olin A. Curtis, *The Christian Faith,* pp. 40-43. Eaton & Mains, New York, 1905.
23. A phrase of John Hutton, *The British Weekly,* May 24, 1928, Article, "Things in General."
24. Psalm 119:101.
25. John 3:19-21.
26. See McClure, *op. cit.,* p. 137. And for "George Eliot's Analysis of Motives" see article under this title by Nathan Sheppard in *Library Magazine of American and Foreign Thought,* New York, Vol. 7, pp. 84-96.
27. Lawrence Hyde, *op. cit.,* pp. 28, 29.
28. *Peer Gynt,* Act IV, Scene 1.
29. Genesis 3:6, 11, 12, 13. In this volume "The Lord" is substituted for "Jehovah" in quotations from the American Standard Version.
30. Rudolph Sohm, *Outlines of Church History,* p. 35. Macmillan, New York, 1895.
31. See *Protestantism,* A Symposium, Commission on Courses of Study, The Methodist Church, Nashville, Tennessee, 1944, especially chapter, "Cardinal Principles of Protestantism," pp. 125-136, by A. C. Knudson. See also Calvin, *Institutes of the Christian Religion,* Presbyterian Board of Education, Philadelphia, Book I, chapter 7; and Luther, *Address to the Nobility of the German Nation,* in *First Principles of the Reformation,* edited by Wace and Buchheim, Lutheran Publishing Society, Philadelphia, 1895, pp. 25-27.
32. Deuteronomy 30:11-14. See Romans 10:8.
33. John Oman, *Vision and Authority.* New and Revised Edition, p. 100. Harper and Brothers, New York, 1929.
34. Theodore Meyer Greene, *Liberal Education Re-examined,* p. 57. Harper and Brothers, New York, 1943.
35. William S. Gray, "A Decade of Progress," *The Teaching of Reading: A Second Report,* p. 16. The Thirty-sixth Yearbook of the National Society for the Study of Education, Part I. Bloomington, Illinois, Public School Publishing Co., 1937. See also William S. Gray, *Reading in General Education,* An Exploratory Study, American Council on Education, Washington, D. C., 1940, pp. 46, 47.
36. See, *e.g.,* Amos 3:7, 8; Isaiah 6:9; 28:23-29; Jeremiah 5:20-29.
37. Theodore Meyer Greene, *The Arts and the Art of Criticism,* p. vii. Princeton University Press, 1940.
38. Dudley and Faricy, *The Humanities,* p. v. McGraw-Hill Book Company, New York, 1940.
39. II Samuel 5:24.
40. Oliver Wendell Holmes, "The Chambered Nautilus," last lines.

ADVENTURING IN FIRSTHAND ACQUAINTANCE

"A very slight knowledge of music will enable
anyone to detect discords in the exquisite harmonies of Haydn or Mozart; and Bentley
has found more false grammar in the Para-
dise Lost than ever poor boy was whipped
for through all the forms of Eton or Westminster; but to know why the minor note is
introduced into the major key, or the nomi-
native case left to seek for its verb, requires
an acquaintance with some preliminary steps
of the Methodical scale, at the top of which
sits the author, and at the bottom the critic."
—S. T. Coleridge.

Adventuring in Firsthand Acquaintance

ह‍

THE NATURE OF ACQUAINTANCE

In *The Courtship of Miles Standish,* when Priscilla smiles and, with eyes overrunning with laughter, says in a tremulous voice, "Why don't you speak for yourself, John?" she is simply bearing witness to the surprised John Alden that there is no such thing in human relations as a secondhand adventure in acquaintance.[1] Our English word *acquaint* is derived from the Latin *accognoscere,* "to know or to recognize perfectly." Acquaintance emphasizes the personal character of cognition. That is to say, it involves experience between people who know something together. Acquaintance, therefore, is an essential term in the language of friendship. Whenever mutuality of understanding is desired, or conversation is to take place, or whenever there is to be communication between person and person, it must occur upon the level of firsthand acquaintance.

When we turn from the language of friendship to the quest for truth, acquaintance retains this same essential quality of firsthand participation. It might well be said that nothing is ever really ours, however it may have been presented to us originally, which we have not personally appropriated or allowed to prove itself in our own experience. Anyone who looks at life seriously must consider the quest for the truth by which he lives in terms of firsthand acquaintance.

There is an old Chinese saying to the effect that "If the wrong man uses the right means, the right means works the wrong way." Even though this be true, it need not deter anyone from making inquiry concerning the right means. When anything is to be done the question *how* is always pertinent, no matter who the performer may be. The formal term in education which provides the answer to this question is the word *method*. Therefore, we may appropriately begin by inquiring into the meaning of method.

THE MEANING OF METHOD

The word *method* is derived directly from the Greek *methodos,* which means literally *a way or path of transit.* Therefore, by derivation, method involves a progressive transition from one step in any course to another. A word often confused with method is system. Hence these terms should be sharply differentiated. "System, though not uncommon in the sense of a fully developed and often carefully formulated method, . . . may often as easily apply to the scheme as to the actual way of doing something."[2] Richard C. Trench removes the ambiguity which ordinarily confuses method with system when he distinguishes between them as follows: "When men say that there is want of method in it [i.e. Scripture], they would speak more accurately if they said there was want of system; for the highest method, even the method of the Spirit, may reign where system there is none. Method . . . is inseparable from the ideas of God and of order; but system . . . is the artificial arrangement by which man brings within his limited ken that which in no other way he would be able to grasp as a whole. That there should be books of systematic Theology,—books with their plan and scheme thus lying on their very surface and meeting us at once,—this is most needful; but most needful is it also that Scripture should not be such a book . . . It is not a defect in Scripture . . . but rather a glory and a prerogative that there reigns in it the freedom and fulness of nature, and not the narrowness and strictness of art."[3] In these lectures we shall not use the word method to refer to any artificial scheme or arrangement.

With this distinction in mind let us seek a more positive definition of method. Observe, first, that we use the word in the singular:

method, not methods. A survey of the various methods by which men have approached Scripture reveals a considerable variety. Terry lists some of these. For instance, he mentions the Halachic and Hagadic methods of the ancient Hebrews; the allegorical method of Philo; the mystical interpretations of Clement and Origen; Swedenborg's science of correspondencies; the accommodation theory of Semler; the moral interpretation of Kant; the naturalistic theory of Paulus; Hegel's dialectical method of thesis, antithesis, and synthesis; the mythical theories of Strauss and Baur; speculative philosophy; dogmatic exposition and apology; and the grammatico-historical method.[4] Much may be learned by comparing and appraising the various methods of studying Holy Scripture through the ages. But we should like to determine, now, the rudimentary essentials of any method.

In doing this we shall not expect to commend any one particular mode of study to the exclusion of others. There is no special bridge over which all wayfarers must pass if they would enter into the inner sanctuary of Scripture. Yet, in a sense, it must be said that in order to move from here . . . to there, one must pass through every intervening point. The former students of Wilbert Webster White will always remember a story of his days in India when working under the Y.M.C.A. among Hindu students. One day, in conversation, a young Hindu said, "I cannot understand why you Christians are always insisting that there is one way to be saved and only one." He was thinking, of course, of the Hindu, the Buddhist, and the Mohammedan ways of life. Then he added, "What difference does it make, for instance, how I get to the second floor of this house; whether I go up the staircase, or take the lift, or climb up a ladder and come in through the window?" "At first," said Dr. White, "I could think of no adequate reply. Then it came in a flash: 'There is only one way to get to the second floor of this house, and that is to overcome gravity!'" What, then, are the essential characteristics of this path of transit called method?

Observe, in the second place, that conceived in its widest possible scope, method is procedure. And the primary consideration in procedure of any kind is that it be suited to the end in view. Experience teaches men that when anything is to be done, some ways are better, certain movements are more effective, than others. This may be illustrated in countless life activities. The novice in almost any field of endeavor discovers after a certain amount of trial and error that he has successfully made a transition from mere effort to a more consciously guided process. In other words, by following a certain order of procedure he achieves his end with greater economy of effort, more proficient application, and a more satisfying degree of success. Broadly speaking, method thus embodies three distinct characteristics. It is procedure with an end in view. It is orderly procedure. It involves a consciously guided effort. M. M. Musselman, in recording memorable incidents in the life of his father, tells us how his father learned to play golf. A new golf course had been laid out near Wichita, Kansas. His father, wishing first to try out the game alone, resorted to practicing secretly. The son describes his father's efforts as follows: "At first he flailed away as though wielding a shinny club. This didn't work; the result was usually a hook or a slice. He tried swinging slow and swinging fast. Nothing worked. Finally he reasoned that if he could swing the club in a perfectly perpendicular arc, with the club face pointed toward the green, the ball would *have* to go straight. The result was a swing the like of which had never before been seen on a golf course. He looked as though he were trying to tie himself into a knot, but the ball *did* go straight."[5] There was no system in his swing, but there was method in it! Method is the conscious accommodation of an individual's powers to the requirements of a situation, attaining the end in view by orderly procedure which involves a consciously guided effort.

But to these characteristics now still another may be added. Since method is a consciously guided, orderly process it must allow for the full play of those strictly personal qualities which distinguish one individual from another. To subordinate individual qualities to artificial rules or standards is system. To call forth into fullest possible expression those native powers of personality which distinguish an individual from his fellows is method. There are as many different ways of doing things as there are individuals. But this does not mean that the accommodation of one's powers to the requirements of a situation is entirely without a measure of control. Two factors in practical experience provide for this control: first, the taking of certain steps which achieve order and give unity to experience; and second, the recognition of those factors which maintain and foster conditions of growth. The Christian life is a growing life. When a Christian ceases to grow he has really ceased to live. No conception of method, even its broadest scope of reference, could possibly be considered complete which does not include these two elements of control in personal experience. "Method at bottom," says John Dewey, "is but the way of doing things in any given case . . . It will indicate . . . the main steps that have to be taken, and suggest the crucial points where conditions of growth have to be maintained and fostered."[6]

We are now prepared to summarize what we have been saying. Method is orderly procedure within a consciously guided process which calls into full play the distinctive personal capacities and aptitudes of an individual. These distinctive personal qualities are aided and controlled when the individual recognizes and practices certain main steps of procedure and eliminates whatever does not cultivate conditions of growth.

We may profitably examine with greater care the precise relation between these so-called main steps to be taken and the crucial points where conditions of growth have to be maintained and fostered.

ILLUSTRATIONS OF METHOD

Any competent physician called upon to treat a sick person knows that if the patient is to be made well nature must do the healing. All the physician can do is to co-operate with nature. All his skill and

medical knowledge avail nothing unless they aid and abet the healing process itself. He himself cannot supply the vitality necessary
to health, but he can help the patient to fulfill the conditions by
which vitality can be released for healing. There are certain essential steps, however, which the physician can and must take. For
instance, diagnosis precedes prescription. Examination of the patient for symptoms is the first stage of co-operation with nature.
Different physicians may follow individual modes of approach in
determining these symptoms, but in any case they will include the
temperature of the patient, his pulse beat, respiration, blood pressure, and so on. Why these particular factors? Simply because
every one of them is vital to health. Each has a bearing on diagnosis, and therefore upon prescription. Each involves a crucial point
where conditions of growth must be fostered if the patient is to be
healed.

Or let us take an illustration from agriculture. Any experienced
farmer knows that if he is to reap a crop, nature must do the growing. All he can do is to co-operate with nature. There are certain
main steps which, if taken in season and in order, provide those
conditions by which growth of the crop may be assisted. Plowing
precedes planting, and so do harrowing and fertilizing. The first
steps are those which prepare the soil for the seed. Once the soil
has been prepared, the farmer may plant with expectation. But
planting must be followed by cultivating before there can be reaping
and threshing and before the golden grain is ready for the bin. Still
other steps are necessary before the grain is ready for the kitchen
and the table and the family. The farmer plows and plants but nature gives the increase.

The physician and the process of healing, the farmer and the
process of growth, provide practical illustrations of vital method.
Healing and growth in the natural world have their analogy in
the spiritual realm. Scripture abounds in imagery which illustrates
both. Jeremiah asks, "Is there no balm in Gilead? is there no physician there? why then is not the health of the daughter of my

people recovered?"[7] Isaiah uses the imagery of husbandry in his parable of the plowman who harrows and sows, but looks to the Lord of Hosts "who is wonderful in counsel, and excellent in wisdom" to bless his labors with fruitage.[8] Jesus employs similar imagery in His parable of the Soils.[9] The seed in the word. The soils represent so many degrees of fulfillment or non-fulfillment of conditions of growth. Paul affirms the same idea in describing his ministry to the Corinthians: "I planted, Apollos watered; but God gave the increase."[10] The pastoral counsel in II Timothy refers to the same concept, but with slightly different imagery, in the words, "But abide thou in the things which thou hast learned and hast been assured of, knowing of whom thou hast learned them; and that from a babe thou hast known the sacred writings which are able to make thee wise unto salvation through faith which is in Christ Jesus."[11] Thus Scripture utilizes the freedom and fullness of nature to describe the method of spiritual culture.

How the Scriptures make wise unto salvation is not our immediate quest. In keeping with the announced purpose of these studies our primary concern now is not with the nature of revelation but with the method of response. We have described this response as an adventure in firsthand acquaintance. This adventure means fulfilling conditions whereby what is vital in Scripture fosters and maintains growth in Christian stature. Henry More long ago suggested that "nothing can be brought to any great beauty, order, fulness nor maturity without our industry—nor indeed with it, unless the dew of divine grace descend upon it, without whose blessing this culture will thrive as little as the labor of the husbandman without showers of rain."[12]

THE CRUCIAL POINTS OF RESPONSE

What, then, are the crucial points of response which determine the main steps to be taken in method? Let us state and examine four tests of such response.

The Activity of Commitment

When any course of action is contemplated one of the primary factors involved is the attitude of the actor. This is true not only of the specific type of activity we have in mind when we consider the fitness of Scripture for unfolding the spiritual life of men; it is an essential factor in the very constitution of man. "Both as a biological organism, and as a human being, man must repeatedly commit himself to some specific course of action," declares Theodore Meyer Greene. And he continues, "He is forever being confronted with alternatives between which he must choose, and each decision entails its own inescapable consequences. As a physical being he must adapt himself to his physical environment if he is to continue to exist . . . As a social being man is under a similar necessity to act and to abide by the consequences of his actions . . . But man is also a being sensitive to moral values and capable of a religious response to the supernatural. This again involves a series of concrete decisions whose moral implications are far-reaching and inescapable . . . Thus participation and commitment are unavoidable in all practical affairs, in the pursuit of happiness, and in the realization of moral and religious ends."[13] How, then, do participation and commitment enter into the adventure of firsthand acquaintance with Scripture?

Here two types of approach are possible. Professor Warner Fite distinguishes between them as the activity of agent and the activity of observer. "In comparing the various modes of viewing human action and experience there is no contrast more striking than that furnished by viewing a situation from within as agent and viewing it from without as observer . . . between having an experience and contemplating the expression of such an experience."[14] According to this contrast an agent is any person who participates at firsthand in any given situation and contemplates the object of his attention with sympathetic understanding based upon immediate intuition. On the other hand, the observer views his object from without, in the spirit of cold, dispassionate inquiry.

The bearing of these contrasted attitudes is well illustrated in Tolstoy's conversation with his friend Ivan Turgenev about a horse. One day while he and Turganev were taking a walk they came to an old worn-out horse grazing in a field. Tolstoy went up to the horse and stroked it and began to give voice to its thoughts and sad feelings so vividly and convincingly that Turgenev at last exclaimed, "I am sure, Leo Nikolayevich, you must once have been a horse yourself!"[15] Tolstoy's capacity to enter into the inner being of an old horse involved the activity of the agent. Had he instead discussed the horse with Turgenev as a veterinarian, or as a horse trader, his approach would have been that of the observer. Tolstoy's interest was not professional, detached, separated, or external. It was directed intuitively toward the living essence of the animal.

If there is to be growth in enlightenment and understanding in his response to Scripture the individual must of course play the role of observer. For it is only by sufficient detachment that he can gain an adequate perspective of Christian truth. As an observer his interest may be directed fruitfully to the relation of the truths of Christianity to those of other religions (the field of Comparative Religions); or to rival statements of truth (Apologetics); or to their adaptiveness to the necessities of human nature (Psychology of Religion); or to historic origins (Historical Criticism); or to their contributions to Christian faith and life (Biblical Theology); or to their congruity with the natural and physical sciences (Systematic Theology). In each case let it be emphasized that the role of the individual is clearly that of an observer. The greater his detachment, the more complete his objectivity, the more effectively will he earn the benefits which come from breadth of view, range of knowledge, and freshness of learning. But let him not confine himself to this role, lest by his one-sided concentration upon the concrete external aspects of his Biblical subject matter he reduce his approach to one of arid intellectualism. It is only as he adopts the role of agent that the observer can truly gain depth of experience, definiteness of purpose, and that freshness of insight which is the mother of wisdom. These are the factors which operate most essentially in contributing to vital spiritual culture. As Professor Fite has shown so convincingly, "The observer as observer is confronted with brute facts which compel his acceptance; for the agent, on the other hand, whatever is accepted must also in some sense be chosen."[16] Mark that word *chosen*. What makes a response to Scripture genuine is continually repeated commitment. This activity is not essentially different from the attitude prescribed by artistic contemplation, since Scripture is presented in the form of composition and thus is to be approached as are all other writings. The individual in the role of agent adopts the attitude of active commitment by seeking immediacy of impression united with that warmth and intimacy which come only through firsthand participation.

It might be argued that in this dual role the individual must delay his activity as agent until he has first achieved that breadth of view and objectivity of impression which come from the observer's quest. Thus he would be intelligently equipped for the more intimate role of agent. Or it might be said that the two roles must in effect be simultaneous in practical experience and that it is the Christian's business to see that they are kept in proper balance. To both of these suggestions one might reply as Professor Greene does, that "action and passion, not comprehension of what the situation signifies, is the dominant motif of firsthand participation in human affairs."[17] Only by conscious choice as agent does a man really enter into the inner sanctuary of Scripture. What makes his response effective in personal life is his attitude of possession. Not content with the knowledge about Biblical subject matter that his activity as observer may bring him, the individual begins and continues his quest as agent. Like other artistic activities the individual's attitude toward Christian truth is one of love, with a view to possessing the object of his attentions, and it involves a corresponding surrender of self on his own part. His interest in Christian truth must be so complete that it amounts to an irresistible and passionate urge to make it a personal possession. Francis Thompson grasped this primal condition of winning truth, and expressed it suggestively in his lines:

> "Truth is a maid whom men woo diversely,
> This as a spouse; that as a light-'o-love,
> To know, and having known, to make his brag.
> But woe to him that takes the immortal kiss,
> And not estates her in his housing life,
> Mother of all his seed! So he betrays
> Not truth, the unbetrayable, but himself."[18]

Jesus also recognized and stressed this distinctive quality among those who would be His disciples. In responding to the first question addressed to Him by His earliest disciples, "Teacher, where abidest thou?" He said unto them, "Come, and ye shall see."[19] The gateway to the reality of Christian truth enshrined in Scripture bears the universal invitation, "Come, and ye shall see." Self-commitment, firsthand participation, is the first main step of method. It is as active agent that the individual enters and continues the quest for illumination that is distinctively Christian. It is only as he strains his ear to catch overtones to which he has previously paid little attention, trains his eye to detect the concealed wonders and choicest treasures of Scripture, determines to abandon some of his most cherished preconceptions and expose himself to hitherto unfaced truths, that he both fosters and maintains conditions of growth.

The Art of Observing

A second main step of method, corresponding to a similar crucial point of growth, is the art of observing. Participation in any course of action involves not only the attitude of the actor, but also definite efforts on his part. He must do some things for himself which no one else can do for him. If the infant does not learn to use his feet he will never learn to walk. At this point every individual is a pioneer. He must learn, at whatever cost, to stand upon his own feet. If participation and commitment are unavoidable in all practical affairs, the ability to discern is decisive in fostering conditions of personal growth. And this is no less imperative in spiritual than in practical affairs. Failure very often follows commitment to a course of action simply because the individual does not see with his own eyes, or hear with his own ears. This does not mean that he is either blind or deaf, but primarily that he has not paid attention. Whether he does pay attention is in some measure the test of his commitment. Has he really chosen to make the word of truth his own personal possession? In the penetrating analysis entitled *Vision and Authority,* John Oman declares, "We truly inherit nothing except what we also discern. Nothing is ours, however it may be presented to us, except *we* discover its truth and except it prove itself again in *our* experience . . . Mere acceptance of the conclusions of others . . . is not the way by which we . . . lay broad and deep foundations. With eyes bandaged in formulas men see only the aspect of life the formula allows . . . They grow accustomed to the half-light . . . and with all the colors of it toned down to suit the sombre hues of a twilight soul."[20] But once let an individual determine to flood his twilight with genuine illumination—really to see—off must come the bandages! He must learn to look with his own eyes. The art of observing has its roots so deep in personality, and its importance for growth in Christian stature is so vital, that we propose to devote the following chapter to it. We pause here only long enough to indicate that this art of observing is essentially a work—the work of re-creation.

The Work of Re-creation

Two direct types of genuine experience are possible to every individual. The first is creation, the second is re-creation. For instance Handel, when referring to his experience in composing the Hallelujah Chorus, declared, "I did think I did see all Heaven before me and the great God Himself."[21] Here he speaks of himself in the work of creating—a role comparatively few individuals are equipped to perform. But when once a genius has created a work it must be re-created by the many. As a work of musical composition the Hallelujah Chorus comes to us with a specific subject matter, form, and content so vibrant, so real, that it evokes an immediate, thrilling response. Although we may not see the gates of heaven open when we hear it, at least we never listen to the Hallelujah Chorus seated. There is that in the music which impels an audience to rise to its feet whenever the opening chords are sounded. The degree of re-creative experience enjoyed upon hearing this inspired music depends upon the capacity and skill of each individual in the audience to re-create for himself the experience mediated to him by the composer. What is true in music is true of all the arts. They are but the media by which the realities represented are disclosed to the sympathetic audience or individual. Like the other arts, literature also must be re-created. And the Holy Scriptures, since their medium of expression is that of literature, call for a similar mode of response. The re-creation of literature, however, must be distinguished from the re-creation of the other arts.

Professor Greene states the distinction as follows: "Literature is unique among the arts . . . in possessing a dual primary medium, which is essentially symbolic in character. That is, the visible symbols . . . and the sounds which are uttered must then be associated with their appropriate symbolized meanings, for the literary work to come into existence as an object awaiting artistic apprehension and appraisal."[22] This dual character of literature may be illustrated in terms of a language not understood by a reader. For instance, he may hear the words of the original and get the sound without the sense; or he may hear a translation and get the sense without the sound. In neither case has he really come to know the whole work as it should be known. But even though everyone who hears something read in his own language gets the sound, only those get the meaning who apprehend inwardly the sense conveyed by the symbols. Professor Greene says that in every adequate response to a literary work there are two distinct acts of the imagination. These acts, he says, "often take place simultaneously and are always ultimately fused," but for the purpose of analysis "can be distinguished by entitling the first the 'reconstructive' and the second the 're-creative' . . . It is the historical critic's primary task to facilitate accurate reconstruction in the light of historical evidence, whereas the re-creative critic's task is to help us to re-create with artistic comprehension what has been correctly reconstructed."[23]

This analysis now prepares the way for dealing with a matter of acute importance in Biblical studies. The problem may be phrased in the form of a question: What is the relation between historical and re-creative study? That this is a matter of supreme concern is indicated by the confusion which exists generally in the minds of many earnest Christians concerning the use of the word *criticism* in connection with the Bible. In theological education *criticism* has a precise meaning. It refers to Old Testament and New Testament Introduction: the process of determining the historical origin, preservation, integrity, and transmission of the several books of the Bible. Only by this approach may a sufficient comprehension of Biblical revelation in its historical setting be acquired.

It is here that the humanities now provide a valuable answer to our question. Professor Greene has shown convincingly that historical criticism is only one of three necessary aspects of criticism in the adequate appraisal of any work: the historical, the re-creative, and the judicial. Each of these aspects of criticism relates itself to "a corresponding aspect of the work of art itself—historical criticism, to the work's historical character and orientation; re-creative criticism, to its unique artistic individuality; and judicial criticism, to its artistic value." These aspects of criticism are not mutually exclusive but rather "are mutually conditioning factors of a single organic process."[24]

Study of the Bible in its historical setting has value primarily in aiding every man to "reconstruct" the situation out of which the several books of the Bible, as well as the whole collection, came. This, however, is not sufficient for a competent judicial comprehension of Holy Scripture. For the word of truth becomes the word of faith, only as it is inwardly and then outwardly re-created in a man's being. Paul phrased it in this way: "The word is nigh thee, in thy mouth, and in thy heart: that is the word of faith, which we preach."[25] The factually-minded student of Scripture must, therefore, complete his learning by cultivating a sharp and active use of his re-creative powers, while the person whose re-creative powers are keen and alert must not fail to keep his studies historically grounded by adequate reconstruction. However, as Professor Greene reminds us, we must differentiate between the logical and the psychological order of these two necessary activities in study. Historical inquiry logically precedes the re-creative, as its necessary condition, because a work, "especially when it belongs to another age or culture" as the Bible does, "simply cannot be understood without the requisite historical orientation. Re-creation in turn is the necessary (although insufficient) condition of judicial appraisal, since only that can be significantly appraised whose nature has been re-creatively apprehended. Psychological interest tends to reverse this order. We normally take pains to re-create what, at first glance, arouses our artistic interest . . . and historical research in the realm of art is usually motivated by the desire to understand more adequately what we have already partially re-created and enjoyed."[26]

If method is orderly procedure, when is the logical order to be given priority in the Christian response, and when the psychological? The answer will depend upon the purpose of the student. When breadth of view or range of knowledge is desired, the logical order normally takes precedence over the psychological. In seeking the requisite historical orientation the student will be expected to gather and interpret "available biographical, social, cultural, and other types of evidence" which bear upon the particular parts of Scripture he is studying. Only in the light of such studies can the student come to understand and feel the functional relation of the Scriptures to the growing experience of the ancient Hebrew and early Christian communities. But the Scriptures come alive for him with real urgency as the word of the living God only as they function *in* him. He must go on to complete his enlarging view by consciously choosing to make this word his own personal possession. A young Chinese student wrote to his teacher about the intellectual and spiritual tensions which accompanied his study of Biblical criticism, saying that it was an experience which left his mind bewildered and his inner hungers unsatisfied. "But," he added with genuine discernment, "I have found new light in Holy Scripture since I began reading and behaving it!" "Behaving" Scripture is the equivalent of the re-creative method. This is what has been referred to appropriately as "cottage wisdom and faith," where practical rather than academic necessities prevail; where vital issues must be acted on as well as comprehended; and where psychological necessity takes precedence over logical order. Thus re-creation is work. It is the process by which the individual apprehends and identifies the expressed intent in the medium he is studying. And this expressed intent now becomes the initiative of his own response. The objective requirements of truth as revealed in this medium are matched by an equally objective response on the part of the whole man.

So far we have considered three tests which may be applied to any adventure in firsthand acquaintance—tests which are equally valid when applied to the study of the Bible. First, how far is the student summoned into actual participation as agent? Second, what provision is made for firsthand observation? Third, how truly are historical and re-creative procedures balanced?

Maintaining Continuity of Quest

And now we may consider briefly a fourth test. Is continuity of quest achieved? The human mind has an almost incurable bent for making snap judgments. We leap before we look. We think and act without adequate forethought. We settle down into grooves of thought and conduct from which we do not like to be disturbed. It is unlikely that steady advance in the learning process will be made apart from such a consciously guided process as we have been discussing. Continuity of quest requires that the center of the learning experience be kept vital and dynamic. Two mutually dependent modes of approach to truth are available. To utilize either to the exclusion or disadvantage of the other is to confuse and unbalance one's mental processes. One is induction, the other deduction. Induction considers a succession of observed facts and draws from them a general conclusion. Deduction, having reached a general conclusion, applies that conclusion to an unknown case or a new situation. The process called induction, therefore, is the "logic of discovery," deduction the "logic of proof." "Induction," as Herman Harrell Horne suggests, "is the beginning of the process of knowledge which deduction completes." He points out that had not Aristotle been such a wide observer, "and had he not thus provided his successors with so many general principles, the Middle Age period of deduction would have been shorter . . . Dogmatic minds, trusting to the perfection of the deductive syllogism, tend to forget that their major premises are all inductive conclusions and are thus tinged with the element of probability . . . Literature and history have usually been taught deductively; they need to be taught inductively more."[27] That word *more* might well be underscored when these two mutually dependent modes of procedure are considered in relation to Biblical studies if continuity is to be properly maintained in participation, firsthand observation, and the work of re-creation.

Let us conclude by drawing a practical illustration from the arts. The art of wood engraving may seem to be a far cry from the study of the Bible. But in terms of method the relation is very close. Before our modern mechanical processes came into use all pictures, from the cheapest advertisements to the finest illustrations, had to be engraved on wood before they could be reproduced. The name of Timothy Cole ranks high among American wood engravers. His younger days were not without struggle, for he rejected traditional, static methods of wood engraving, and so came into conflict with the Old School. He insisted that a reproduction of a painting must be a re-creation—a re-creation which gave as clearly as possible all the characteristics of the original even if traditional rules of procedure had to be sacrificed. According to his biographer, no wood engraver before Cole had ever realized with such truth the characteristics of the particular paintings he represented in his woodcuts. He even endeavored to give the sensation of the artist's visible brush strokes, and his work was so realistic that before long it was being imitated by many others.

After his reputation had been well established Timothy Cole wrote these illuminating lines, descriptive of his growing re-creative experience as a wood engraver. Speaking of his earlier days he says: "In those days I merely thought of engraving. Now the *engraving* is nothing—absolutely nothing. It is the reproduction of the original alone that concerns me. Away with your nonsense of textures and stuff. Unless they contribute toward a more faithful reproduction of the original, they are rubbish. The engraver must work in the spirit of the true artist . . . must stand aside, make way for the artist. Must not speak his own words, nor do his own works, nor think his own thoughts, but must be the organ through which the mind of the artist speaks."[28] Here Timothy Cole has given us a true picture of the re-creative interpreter who fulfills the conditions of firsthand acquaintance. His fidelity to the expressed intention of the great masters made him an effective organ of interpretation. The greatness of the works he so faithfully re-created made him great, and he could say:

> "Eternal truth—I have it, man!
> There's nothing fixed save change.
> On this truth may we safely plan
> And build, nor further range!"[29]

NOTES

The quotation on the title page of this chapter is from S. T. Coleridge's *Treatise on Method,* Edited by Alice D. Snyder, p. 32.

1. *The Complete Poetical Works of H. W. Longfellow,* p. 171. Houghton, Mifflin Co., New York, 1893. "The Courtship of Miles Standish," III, last lines.
2. *Webster's Dictionary of Synonyms,* p. 546. G. & C. Merriam Co., Springfield, Massachusetts, 1942. For an illuminating discussion of Method, see S. T. Coleridge's *Treatise on Method,* Edited by Alice D. Snyder, pp. 1-11. Constable & Co., London, 1934.
3. Richard C. Trench, Hulsean Lectures, 1845, pp. 92, 93.
4. Milton S. Terry, *Biblical Hermeneutics, pp.* 58-70. Eaton and Mains, New York, 1911. See also F. W. Farrar, *The History of Interpretation.* E. P. Dutton and Co., New York, 1886.
5. M. M. Musselman, *Wheels in His Head,* p. 54. Whittlesey House, New York, 1946. Quoted by permission of the publisher.
6. *A Cyclopedia of Education,* Edited by Paul Monroe, Macmillan, New York, 1911. Article, "Method," by John Dewey, pp. 202-205. The whole reference is as follows: "Strictly speaking, method is thoroughly individual. Each person has his own instinctive way of going at a thing; the attitude and the mode of approach and attack are individual. To ignore this individuality of approach, to try to substitute for it, under the name of 'general method,' a uniform scheme of procedure, is simply to cripple the only effective agencies of operation, and to overlay them with a mechanical formalism that produces only a routine conventionality of mental quality. Certain features may be found, however, which are involved in the transition from unconscious effort to a more consciously guided process. These features may be abstracted and generalized. While the outcome will not put individuals in possession of a sure key to intellectual efficiency, it will indicate to a teacher the main steps that have to be taken, and suggest the crucial points where conditions of growth have to be carefully maintained and fostered." Used by permission of the publisher.
7. Jeremiah 8:22.
8. Isaiah 28:23-29.
9. Mark 4:1-20; Matthew 13:1-23; Luke 8:4-15.
10. I Corinthians 3:6.
11. II Timothy 3:14, 15.
12. Henry More, *The Mystery of Godliness,* Book I, Chapter 2.
13. Theodore Meyer Greene, *The Arts and the Art of Criticism,* pp. 236, 237.
14. Warner Fite, *The Living Mind,* p. 24. The Dial Press, New York, 1930.
15. See Aylmer Maude, *The Life of Tolstoy,* The World's Classics, Vol. II, Later Years, p. 24.
16. Warner Fite, *op. cit.,* p. 36.
17. Theodore Meyer Greene, *op. cit.,* p. 239.
18. *The Complete Poetical Works of Francis Thompson.* The Modern Library, p. 156. "Whereto Art Thou Come?"
19. As reported in John's Gospel, 1:38, 39.
20. John Oman, *Vision and Authority,* p. 58. Harper and Brothers, New York, 1929.

21. See Newman Flower, *George Frideric Handel, His Personality and His Times*, p. 271. Cassell and Co., New York, 1923. "The whole of *Messiah* from beginning to end was set upon paper in twenty-four days. Considering the immensity of the work and the short time involved, it will remain, perhaps for ever, the greatest feat in the history of musical composition. It was the achievement of a giant inspired—the work of one who, by some extraordinary mental feat, had drawn himself completely out of the world, so that he dwelt—or believed he dwelt—in the pastures of God . . . He did not leave the house; his man-servant brought him food, and as often as not returned in an hour to the room to find the food untouched, and his master staring into vacancy. When he had completed Part II, with the 'Hallelujah Chorus,' his servant found him at the table, tears streaming from his eyes. 'I did think I did see all Heaven before me, and the great God Himself!' he exclaimed . . . For twenty-four days he knew those uplands reached only by the higher qualities of the soul."

22. Theodore Meyer Greene, *op. cit.*, p. 350.

23. *Ibid.*, p. 352.

24. *Ibid.*, p. 369, 370.

25. Romans 10:8.

26. Theodore Meyer Greene, *op. cit.*, p. 373.

27. Herman Harrell Horne, *Psychological Principles of Education*, pp. 179-184. Macmillan, New York, 1925.

28. Alphaeus P. Cole, and Margaret Ward Cole, *Timothy Cole, Wood Engraver*, Limited Edition, Illustrated with nineteen of Timothy Cole's finest wood engravings, p. 80. The Pioneer Associates, New York, 1935.

29. *Ibid.*, p. 81.

OPENING THE EYES OF THE UNDERSTANDING

"In my judgment, your first care should be to
learn to observe . . . Do you see the thing
exactly as it is? Do you strip away from it
your own likings and dislikings, your own
previous notions of what it ought to be? Do
you come face to face with things?"
—George Herbert Palmer.

"A man must see before he can say . . . At first
blush, a man is not capable of reporting
truth. To do that he must be drenched and
saturated with it. Then truth will exhale
from him naturally."
—Henry David Thoreau.

THREE

Opening the Eyes of the Understanding

ह≈

THE RELATION BETWEEN SIGHT AND INSIGHT

JESUS made a very discerning observation about the blindness of the multitudes when He said, "Therefore speak I to them in parables; because seeing they see not, and hearing they hear not, neither do they understand."[1] Being a wise and shrewd observer Jesus recognized the intimate relation between sight and insight; between the use of one's senses and the power to understand. Like the prophets, He accommodated His mode of teaching to the requirements of His hearers. If His disciples were to understand they must really see and hear. "Take heed . . . how ye hear," was one of his favorite words of counsel.[2] "Go and tell John the things which ye have seen and heard," was His reply to the Baptist's disciples who came to Him with John's question, "Art thou he that cometh, or look we for another?"[3] Training the eye to truth's exact severity was the price Jesus knew men must pay if they were to understand.

Louis Agassiz was without doubt one of the world's greatest naturalists, yet, when asked what he regarded as his greatest work he replied, "I have taught men to observe."[4] Like Jesus, Agassiz recognized the primacy of observation in the learning process, and the reason is obvious. Although man is a sentient being he is notoriously unobservant. Comparatively few individuals use what sight they have to the best advantage. Really to see requires concentration. And concentration involves a self-discipline which unfortunately many individuals are not prepared to exert. This failure of the eye to see has been described by Harry Hibbard Kemp:

"The spring blew trumpets of color,
  Her green sang in my brain;
I heard a blind man groping
  'Tap - tap' with his cane.

"I pitied him his blindness—
  But can I say 'I see'?
Perhaps there walks a spirit,
  Close by, that pities me;

"A spirit that hears me tapping
  The five-sensed cane of mind,
Amid such unguessed glories
  That I am worse than blind."[5]

Stirred by the mounting bewilderment of the world today, Richard Guggenheimer sees how this characteristic blindness of the multitudes is related to our widespread confusions. He suggests that at least one way of correcting these grave misunderstandings is to bestir men "to a livelier, fuller, more mature capacity for the visual arts . . . It is a shame," he declares, "that so many of us see much less than is visible. If a man could buy a pair of spectacles guaranteed to reveal everything to him in a far more wonderful light than he had known before, he would rush to purchase them. If a man can learn to see more than he now sees, and see further, and see more beauty, and see more clearly the shape of his own destiny, then he should not hesitate to start learning."[6]

The practical importance of this relation between sight and insight is indicated, furthermore, by the requirements of communication. Robert Louis Stevenson once remarked that the noblest passage he remembered having read in any modern author, and the one most useful to him personally, was the phrase of Thoreau: "It takes two to speak the truth—one to speak and one to hear."[7] What complicates this speaking-hearing process is a third factor which Thoreau does not mention; namely, the medium of communication.

The spoken word must at the same time be a heard word. The written word must also be a seen word. Communication between persons takes place only when what is spoken is actually heard; when what is written is really seen. The senses serve as windows of the understanding.

Coleridge called words "the wheels of the intellect . . ." "Words, . . ." he said, "are living powers; powers by which the things of most importance to mankind are actuated, combined, and humanized."[8] It follows that the measure of one's understanding will depend upon the kind of words he allows to reside in his mind and the kind of attention he gives to them. The Psalmist, meditating upon God and His ways, rightly said, "The opening of thy words giveth light; it giveth understanding unto the simple."[9] The revisers correctly changed the word of the King James translators at this place from "the entrance of thy words" to "the opening of thy words." The Hebrew word translated "opening" literally means "door"; that is, an unfolding or an unveiling. The word translated "simple" in this sentence comes from the same root, so that the sentence might well be expressed: "The unfolding of thy words giveth light; it giveth understanding to the open-minded." Words of divine revelation make their first impression upon the senses. Thus apprehended they become living powers to influence and actuate human personality. Agreeing with this view of the Psalmist, Coleridge spoke of the understanding as the entire power of perceiving and conceiving, "the power of dealing with the impressions of sense, and of composing them into wholes."[10] To see life steadily and see it whole is a work of the understanding. Sharpened senses and the power to understand are intimately connected.

Every experience which involves deeper insight into truth is essentially a test of a person's integrity. Will he summon his own inherent capacities to discern or will he fall back upon some less direct mode of apprehension supplied from without? Assistance at some points may occasionally be necessary, but if a man in his intellectual life comes to rely upon external helps as a final authority upon which to base his own views, or if he allows the views of others to become the mainspring of his actions, he thereby cripples rather than advances his own growth. He stultifies rather than matures his spiritual stature. In such matters, as John Oman has rightly observed, "the help of others is essential, but the authority of others is stagnation."[11]

THE NATURE OF AESTHETIC RESPONSE

We may now appropriately consider the nature of the aesthetic response which has such a vital bearing upon understanding.

Two friends were once overheard in conversation before a picture in an art museum. One was heard to say, "But it's not a Cimabue!" The other asked, "How do you know it's not a Cimabue?" To which the first replied, "Because I am always silent in the presence of a Cimabue." Commenting upon this bit of fatuous conversation, William M. Ivins, Jr., former Curator of Prints at the Metropolitan Museum of Art in New York, has suggested that the two words "always silent" disguise two basic ideas concerning aesthetic experience. "The word *always*," he says, "indicates the idea that the only, and therefore the best, way for anyone to gain acquaintance with a work of art is through looking so often and so hard at it that he acquires an easy and familiar acquaintance with it. The word *silent* indicates the idea that no one can convey by words any conception of the unique and peculiar qualities that make a work of art either the work of a particular artist or a masterpiece. While many things about an object can be explained or adequately stated in words, as for example that it was made by A for B for use in a certain way at a certain time, the essential things about it as art can only be learned or known through firsthand and sensuous experience of it and cannot be phrased in words—which is to say that they cannot be explained."[12]

Any experienced teacher understands this. After offering a valid explanation of a problem, he hears the student say: "I still don't see it that way." And what the student says is perfectly true. He does not comprehend, because it has been explained and not seen. "Once and for all," insists Theodore Meyer Greene, "theoretical analysis (i.e. explanation) is no substitute for immediate aesthetic response or sensitive critical re-creation."[13] Explanations phrased in words can never adequately reveal essential qualities in an object waiting to be discerned.

THE SCIENTIFIC APPROACH TO TRUTH

The nature of aesthetic experience has a corresponding parallel in the scientific approach to truth. In discussing the nature of explanations, P. W. Bridgman describes three types of situation in the scientific quest for truth which have a striking similarity to aesthetic or moral experience. The first is one in which explanation consists merely in disentangling complexities, because it involves no elements in the situation with which a person is unfamiliar. The second is one in which a blockade to understanding is caused by the introduction of unfamiliar elements in a novel situation. "Such a situation constitutes an explanatory crisis and explanation has to stop by definition." The third type of situation cannot be satisfied by an explanation until something happens within the individual. "We may try to force our explanations into a predetermined mold, by formally erecting or inventing beyond the range of present experiment ultimates more or less like elements already familiar to us, and seek to explain all present experience in terms of those chosen ultimates."[14]

These situations correspond to analogous experiences involved in a growing understanding of Scripture. When apprehension of a passage involves nothing essentially new, but only the disentangling of complexities, one may readily seek the required aid in a commentary on the passage, or by consulting a dictionary or an atlas. Here he should find direct help in clearing up his difficulty. Where new or unfamiliar elements are involved and definition is called for, wider reading or research may be necessary. He may need to ask questions of "someone who knows"—a teacher, a pastor, or a more mature friend. He may seek enlightenment from lectures or books on related fields of study, or in a free exchange of views in group study. In fact, the wider he makes his search and the more objective his questions, the more likely he is to find an explanation which will satisfy the requirements of clear understanding.

But there is a third type of situation where the individual himself, not the evidence which he obtains from without, is the determining factor. It is only when some obstruction within him is removed that Scripture spells out a portentous and satisfying message to his soul. This situation is one which corresponds to what Prof. Bridgman calls a primary explanatory crisis. "Every kitten," says he, "is confronted with such a crisis at the end of nine days. Whenever experience takes us into new and unfamiliar realms, we are to be at least prepared for a new crisis. Now what are we to do in such a crisis? It seems to me that the only sensible course is to do exactly what the kitten does, namely, to wait until we have amassed so much experience of the new kind that it is perfectly familiar to us, and then to resume the process of explanation with elements from our new experience included in our list of axioms."[15]

In the serious study of the Scriptures one does not need to be idle during this waiting period. This is the very time when one's own native powers of inward perception must be brought into full play. A stage has arrived in experience where integrity, the response of the whole man, the very nerve center of Christian experience, is involved and where re-creation is the only ultimate answer to the quest. At such a moment a number of halfway expedients may present themselves. Instead of letting patience have its perfect work, an individual may attempt to force interpretation into the predetermined mold of his old life rather than accepting the inducements or implications of the new. He may do this under the necessity of offering explanations to others, such as in teaching a class, making an address, or even preaching a sermon. The stream of his life thus flows in a channel already cut by his professional duties or opportunities. Or this predetermined mold may take the shape of some cherished but only half-assimilated belief—the sort to which an individual clings with a tenacity almost as strong as life itself. The more strongly he clings, the less susceptible he is to any genuine act of re-creation. Did not Jesus deal with this type of character when He challenged the presuppositions of the Jewish leaders of His day in their almost fanatical adherence to interpretation of the law? Hillel used to say, "The more [study of the] Torah, the more life . . . One who has acquired unto himself words of Torah has acquired for himself the life of the world to come."[16] But Jesus insisted, "Ye search the scriptures, because ye think that in them ye have eternal life; and these are they which bear witness of me; and ye will not come to me, that ye may have life."[17]

If neither of these expedients provides the predetermined mold of explanation the individual may fall back upon still a third measure. He may attempt to resolve the situation in terms of the chosen ultimate of some motive which enables him to whittle down the moral demands of a divine word to the convenience of a cherished practice. Stirred by the failure of certain contemporary prophets to respond to divine disclosures which required decision, action, or obedience, Jeremiah cried, "Who hath stood in the council of Jehovah, that he should perceive and hear his word? . . . if they had stood in my council, then had they caused my people to hear my words, and had turned them from their evil way, and from the evil of their doings."[18] To Jeremiah the moral requirements of divine truth could be satisfied by no mere assent to ethical propositions but only by a change of life, brought about through a dramatic re-enactment of the word *repent.*

These moral requirements for understanding Scripture are seen even more clearly in the example and teaching of Jesus, who lived out in utter fidelity the truth which He taught.

THE EXAMPLE AND TEACHING OF JESUS

Jesus examined the adherence of the leaders of His day to the so-called "tradition of the elders" in these words:

"Ye leave the commandment of God, and hold fast the tradition of men. . . . Full well do ye reject the commandment of God, that ye may keep your tradition. For Moses said, Honor thy father and thy mother; and, He that speaketh evil of father or mother, let him die the death: but ye say, If a man shall say to his father or his mother, That wherewith thou mightest have been profited by me is Corban, that is to say, Given to God; ye no longer suffer him to do aught for his father or his mother; making void the word of God by your tradition, which ye have delivered: and many such like things ye do."[19]

And Jesus concluded these searching words by adding, "For from within, out of the heart of men, evil thoughts proceed." No thoughts are more evil in their influence upon the inward life than those which make a man less susceptible to the requirements of divine truth than he was before. The intimate relation of sight to insight, which makes possible a growing experience genuinely Christian, requires that the individual shall reject secondhand adventures in acquaintance. By the assertion of full Christian manhood he must decide that his understanding of Scripture shall not be found in the explanations of others but in the control of powers resident in his own being. How well Jesus understood and taught the imperative claims of inward sight! In the Sermon on the Mount He said:

"For where thy treasure is, there will thy heart be also. The lamp of the body is the eye: if therefore thine eye be single, thy whole body shall be full of light. But if thine eye be evil, thy whole body shall be full of darkness. If therefore the light that is in thee be darkness, how great is the darkness!"[20]

By speaking of the single eye, Jesus indicated the relation between sight and intention. Where one's treasure is, there is his heart. In personal experience the dictates of the heart control the vision of the eye by coloring or distorting or correcting it. The single eye—that is, the eye controlled by intentions to serve God rather than self—is the same eye which associates God's care of the birds with His provisions for the individual's daily food, and God's clothing of the perishable grass of the field with His provisions for bodily raiment. Jesus bade the common people relieve their anxieties by seeking first God's kingdom.

But Jesus also emphasized the fact that divine revelation authenticates itself only to those souls who maintain this attitude of single-hearted receptivity to its claims:

"And no man, when he hath lighted a lamp, covereth it with a vessel, or putteth it under a bed; but putteth it on a stand, that they that enter in may see the light. For nothing is hid, that shall not be made manifest; nor anything secret, that shall not be known and come to light. Take heed therefore how ye hear: for whosoever hath, to him shall be given; and whosoever hath not, from him shall be taken away even that which he thinketh he hath."[21]

According to Jesus, divine truth like a lighted lamp reveals itself to all who really come into its presence. Recognizing the necessity of a receptive attitude He urged His disciples: "Take heed . . . how ye hear." For by hearing He means being openly receptive and responsive to the light of divine truth. These words of Jesus reveal His profound understanding of human nature, for life demonstrates in manifold ways that whosoever hath receptivity to him shall be given, and whosoever hath not receptivity from him shall be taken away even that which he thinketh he hath.

John Calvin likened the Scriptures to spiritual spectacles which enable those of dulled spiritual sight to attain to a true knowledge of God. But what good would spectacles be, he asked, to blind eyes? To keep his analogy true to the teaching of Scripture, Calvin connected this figure of scriptural spectacles with the testimony of the Spirit.[22] To him and to the Church at large, the word of truth and the Spirit of truth inwardly received by the believer make divine revelation effective in personal experience. Did not Jesus promise His disciples that "when he, the Spirit of truth, is come, he shall guide you into all the truth"?[23]

So we may say that any response to Scripture which is genuinely Christian involves these related factors of sight and insight. Two sources of active awareness resident in every individual play a significant role in this growing capacity to understand. The one is found in the resources of inward sight which he summons into operation by a constant act of integrity—each insight into truth being the operation of the single eye intent upon personal seizure of the divine word, each right response becoming the "vestibule of a new revelation." The other source is found in the promised presence of the divine Spirit sent to guide the individual seeker into all truth. When the individual's native resources of sight are fused with the dynamic word of truth, a creative moment in personal experience has arrived. A new sap begins to rise within him. He finds himself responding to fresh and quickening disclosures of his relations to God and man. Or to change the figure, he realizes that the tide of his life is now drawn by the same boundless powers of the deep from which he has come.

THE CULTIVATION OF DISCIPLINED SENSITIVITY

It is now our task to inquire more fully into still another aspect of our subject: the cultivation of disciplined sensitivity. Richard Guggenheimer has suggested that "a livelier, fuller, more mature capacity for the visual arts" has an appreciable influence in making a person more alive to the beauties of nature and to the wonder of life in general.[24]

In the novel entitled *Héloïse and Abélard,* George Moore describes the change wrought in Héloïse through her reading of Virgil. "Virgil . . . unsealed my eyes," said Héloïse, "and by night and day the skies and seas will be beautiful to me."[25] Mr. Moore goes on to describe another occasion: "The river drew her that day as it did every day; and overlooking it she watched the ducks swimming in it, saying to herself: Virgil does not speak of the beauty of ducks swimming in a river, the softness of their voices and their round, black eyes so intelligent, but I should not have known how beautiful they are when swimming in a river if I had not read Virgil, and might well have lived my life out from birth to death without knowing that ducks swam with their pert tails turned up to the sky. It is strange that he should have no words about water-lilies, yet he taught me to see their great leathery leaves."[26]

This unsealing of her eyes, which opened up a whole new world of wonder for Héloïse, is an indication that the cultivation of visual sensitivity is one of the essential disciplines of personal culture, as well as a primary law of growth. In fact, the primacy of firsthand observation is basic to the scientific as well as to the aesthetic approach to truth.

In his autobiography, Nathaniel Southgate Shaler tells of his initial experiences when he went to Harvard to study science under Agassiz. The famous Swiss scientist assigned him to a small pine table with a rusty tin pan on it in a room crowded with other students. "When I sat me down before my tin pan," says Mr. Shaler, "Agassiz brought me a small fish, placing it before me with the rather stern requirement that I should study it, but should on no account talk to anyone concerning it, nor read anything relating to fishes, until I had his permission so to do. To my inquiry 'What shall I do?' he said in effect: 'Find out what you can without damaging the specimen; when I think that you have done the work I will question you.' In the course of an hour I thought I had compassed that fish; it was rather an unsavory object, giving forth the stench of old alcohol, then loathsome to me, though in time I came to like it. Many of the scales were loosened so that they fell off. It appeared to me to be a case for a summary report, which I was anxious to make and get on to the next stage of the business. But Agassiz, though always within call, concerned himself no further with me that day, nor the next, nor for a week. At first this neglect was distressing . . . but I set my wits to work upon the thing, and in the course of a hundred hours or so, I thought I had done much—a hundred times as much as seemed possible at the start. I got interested in finding out how the scales went in series, their shape, the form and placement of the teeth, etc. Finally I felt full of the subject and probably expressed it in my bearing . . . but no attention came from my master except his cheery 'Good morning.' At length on the seventh day, came the question 'Well?' . . . At the end of an hour's telling, he swung off and away, saying, 'That is not right.' . . . I went at the task anew, discarded my first notes, and in another week of ten hours a day labor I had results which astonished myself and satisfied him . . . I shall never forget the sense of power which this experience brought to me. I had learned the art of comparing objects, which is the basis of the naturalist's work."[27]

Samuel H. Scudder, another of Agassiz's pupils, testifies that his teacher's repeated injunction, "Look, look, look," had an equally rewarding effect upon him. Agassiz's training in the method of observing facts and their orderly arrangement was ever accompanied by the urgent exhortation not to be content with them. "Facts are stupid things," he would say, "until brought into connection with some general law."[28] To gain the ability to detect relations between particular objects of attention the individual must learn to see not only intensely but also impartially.

What is true of the scientific approach to facts is equally valid in the aesthetic approach to truth. Perhaps no single individual illustrates the influence of disciplined sensitivity better than Michelangelo. Emerson relates how the great master "dedicated himself from childhood to his death to a toilsome observation of nature. The first anecdote recorded of him shows him to be already on the right road. Granacci, a painter's apprentice, having lent him when a boy . . . some pencils and colors, he went to the fish market to observe the form and color of fins and of the eyes of fish. In this spirit he devoted himself to the study of anatomy for twelve years . . . The depth of his knowledge in anatomy has no parallel among the artists of modern times . . . When he would begin a statue, he made first on paper the skeleton; afterwards upon another paper, the same figure clothed with muscles."[29] This is one reason why the paintings of Michelangelo give such authentic representations of the living form.

Similarly Ruskin appraises Turner's greatness as a painter of landscapes. He intimates that Turner's ability depended upon no knowledge he had gained in the schools about the science and art of painting. "He had merely accustomed himself," says Ruskin, "to see impartially, intensely and fearlessly."[30] While the common man can never expect to achieve what is possible to the creative genius of a Michelangelo or a Turner, this need not hinder him from cultivating his powers to re-create what genius has already created, by accustoming himself to see "impartially, intensely and fearlessly." His powers of apprehension must be controlled by factors which lie in the nature of the objects to which he gives attention.

We cannot take up at this time the philosophical question involved in the appraisal of values. But we may profitably seek to determine what factors assure the individual that he sees truly and not according to the whims or caprices of a vivid imagination. Disciplined sensitivity means that the individual submits himself to a consciously guided process in observation or, as Professor Greene puts it, to a process which is maintained by "normative" sensitivity. This is to say, his awareness is impartial only to the extent to which the essential qualities of the object to which he attends are actually observed. "We are inescapably normative in all our thought and conduct," observes Professor Greene. "This normative compulsion is not only inescapable, it is essential to profitable historical inquiry and to fruitful artistic re-creation."[31] How then may the individual, bent upon firsthand participation, be assured that he is actually engaged in a process of genuine discovery? How may the serious observer be sure he is not projecting his own desires or ideas into the subject matter before him, but that its integrity as well as his own is being strictly preserved?

Holy Scripture, as we have already seen, has a side which is like all other writings. However much it may differ from them in content, it is like all other writings as a medium of communication. This medium is called composition. Composition, as its Latin derivation signifies, literally means putting several things together to make one thing. Since composition is the process by which any medium of communication is brought into being, that same medium can be correctly understood only in terms of the laws of composition.

THE LAWS OF COMPOSITION

All composition depends upon the selection of appropriate symbols of expression and upon their arrangement in an intelligible order. If there is no meaning to express, no symbols are needed. Appropriate symbols in a given order become the medium by which one person expresses himself to another, and these same symbols in this arrangement are the medium by which the second person understands the first. Good composition is the product of appropriate symbols in an articulate arrangement. Thus, a musician composes an air by putting notes (sounds) together in certain relations; a painter composes a picture by combining colors, hues, lines, shapes, in pleasing relations; and an author composes a piece of literature by arranging words (terms) in sequence (syntax) which conveys meaning. So Holy Scripture took shape as a vehicle of communication, to make its divine truth intelligible.

This correlation of the arts accounts for the fact that a landscape painter had to acknowledge that to sculpture he owed his discernment of the forest secrets, having daily observed the long lines of statues in the corridor of the Royal Academy; a student of Renaissance architecture began for the first time to recognize the pilasters on his own house; a minister affirmed that suggestions for arranging his discourses had come to him from observing the pictorial processes of the painter; a music student revealed that her knowledge of the structural harmonies in musical composition made her aware of hitherto hidden relations in certain passages of Scripture; a builder of houses found that his ability to read the relations specified in a blueprint gave him access to the complexities of structure in one of the prophets.[32]

While there may be some unfortunate individuals incapable of aesthetic response—like the congenitally color-blind who can never know what color is—it is more likely, Professor Greene suggests, that everyone possesses some capacity of this type. "Men certainly differ enormously in native aesthetic sensitivity and in the kind of aesthetic training which they have received."[33] But anyone who bestirs himself to a livelier and fuller capacity for the visual arts will find himself mounting a spiral of continued advance in refinement of perception and empirical discovery.

What, then, are the features of this consciously guided process in the use of the eye which we find in the laws of arrangement? No one has stated them more simply or clearly than John Ruskin in his instructive Essay on Composition.[34] Although he presents these so-called laws primarily to help art students to see nature truly, they apply with equal validity to any adventure in discovery, or in expression. An English story writer, for instance, acknowledged that she got her style from a study of this essay.[35] A teacher of philosophy in a midwestern college always begins his class in Introduction to Philosophy by reading this essay to his students in order to sharpen their powers of perception. While Ruskin has not attempted an exhaustive theoretical analysis, he illustrates and defines in a practical way the simplest laws of arrangement. The use of these laws enables an individual to render himself more sensitive to essential qualities which must be personally discerned.

These nine simple laws of arrangement he entitles respectively:

Principality	Contrast
Repetition	Interchange
Continuity	Consistency
Curvature	Harmony
Radiation	

As the first six of these laws are those most commonly used, they will serve to illustrate how the eye may be guided to recognize essential qualities in the medium under observation.

1. The Law of Principality. This is a law of arrangement in which, in order to achieve unity of impression, one feature is made more prominent by placing the others in subordinate positions. For instance, "Good pictures," says Ruskin, "have always one light larger or brighter than other lights, or one figure more prominent than other figures." This is true in good musical composition, although it is not always easy to discover the dominant note because the composer has skillfully blended it with the subordinate notes which create its harmony. For an illustration of this principle of arrangement in Scripture we may take the parables of Jesus. To arrive at a correct interpretation of the Gospel parables one must determine which single feature is essential and which details are drapery. To make a parable "stand on all fours"; that is, to read significance into all the details (as for instance, to assign some special meaning to the birds in the parable of the Mustard Seed),[36] is to obscure the one thing Jesus was seeking to teach. The law of principality is one available aid in this consciously guided process called method by which the eye recognizes what is central or essential and what is subordinate or contributory.

2. The Law of Repetition. This is a mode of expressing unity in which certain parts imitate or repeat one another. "In many sacred compositions," according to Ruskin, "living symmetry, the balance of harmonious opposites, is one of the profoundest sources of their power." For example, in Raphael's Sistine Madonna, the Pope on one side and the saint on the other, and the two cherubs below, one on each side, are harmoniously balanced in relation to the Madonna. Anything in composition—whether a figure or a column in a painting; or a rhythm or a tone in music; or a word or a phrase in literature—must be repeated if it is to have any importance in the completed work. If nothing is repeated, chaos rather than unity is likely to be the result. Repetition plays a conspicuous role in Biblical

composition. The parallelisms in the Psalms; Isaiah's mounting spiral, "For all this his anger is not turned away, but his hand is stretched out still;"[37] Jeremiah's haunting echoes of the word "return . . . return . . . return";[38] Jesus' repeated use of "Ye have heard that it was said to them of old time . . . but I say unto you," in the Sermon on the Mount;[39] Paul's ingemination of the word "love" in I Corinthians 13; and the solemn refrain, "He that hath an ear, let him hear," in the opening chapters of the Revelation[40]— all are familiar examples in Biblical composition of this second available guide to the eye in the process of firsthand acquaintance.

3. The Law of Continuity. Here unity is achieved by giving some orderly succession to a number of objects more or less similar. And this succession is most interesting when it is connected with some gradual change in the aspect or character of the objects, such as may be seen in the receding pillars of a cathedral aisle in perspective, or mountain promontories one behind the other. In Beethoven's Fifth Symphony, the four rhythmic tones with which the symphony opens would be forgotten were they not so frequently presented in pleasing and varied combinations. What gives the first two chapters of Amos such realistic unity is the effective use of continuity. The formula, "For three transgressions of Damascus, yea, for four," is repeated in relation to Gaza, Tyre, Edom, Ammon, Moab, Judah, and Israel. But in each instance the particular transgressions enumerated differ in degree of malignity, although the same fire of divine judgment devours the palaces. Furthermore, each new stage of the prophet's treatment moves in a gradually narrowing circle until he reaches the transgressor about whom he is most concerned: Israel. Another familiar example where unity of expression is quite obviously achieved by continuity is the eleventh chapter of Hebrews, where the expression "by faith" is used to introduce a whole succession of Old Testament characters, each of whom in his own way demonstrates how faith makes certain to a man's soul the unseen things for which he hopes. The eye trained to recognize continuity as a unifying factor where it is so obvious will be prepared to take

advantage of it as a valuable principle of interpretation where it is less obvious; as, for instance, in the passage on the "sabbath rest" in the fourth chapter of Hebrews.

4. The Law of Curvature. "As curves are more beautiful than straight lines, it is necessary to a good composition," says Ruskin, "that its continuities of object, mass, or colour should be, if possible, in curves, rather than straight lines or angular ones." And what distinguishes graceful from ungraceful curvature consists in "a steady change in the whole line from less to more curvature, or more to less." The corresponding principle in musical dynamics is that of crescendo and diminuendo. In literature this law is known as climax. Good narrative must lead from a lesser to a higher, or even to a highest point of interest, in order to reveal an author's intention. This may be done by proceeding from cause to effect or from effect to cause. In the New Testament Luke is the great master of climax. His account of Jesus' visit to the synagogue of Nazareth[41] is arranged about two cycles of cause and effect. His account of Jesus' controversy with the Pharisees in Capernaum,[42] although based on Mark, has its own distinguishing features which trace the rising animosity of the Pharisees until we read that they were "filled with madness; and communed one with another what they might do to Jesus." In chapter 8 Luke deliberately changes Mark's chronological order by recording the visit of Jesus' mother and His brethren after, rather than before, the parables of the Sower and of the Lamp and the Stand, in order to rise to a climax in emphasizing the necessity both of hearing and doing the will of God.[43] Anyone whose eye has learned to observe the relation of cause to effect and, more particularly, of effect to cause will find his reading of Paul's Epistle to the Romans greatly enhanced.

5. The Law of Radiation. "The most simple and perfect connection of lines," Ruskin says, "is by radiation; that is, by their all springing from one point, or closing towards it . . . The boughs of trees, though they intersect and play amongst each other irregularly, indicate by their general tendency their origin from one root . . .

This law of radiation . . . is perhaps, of all principles of composition, the most influential in producing the beauty of groups of form." The 119th Psalm is an excellent example of the law of radiation. Its twenty-two clusters of verse, arranged in acrostic order, are pervaded by one thought: the incomparable excellence of God's law. This single idea, although molded by an almost monotonous sentence structure throughout, is developed with such surpassing variety of expression that, at the end of one's reading, the Psalm as a whole stands out like a stately tree whose boughs, branches, leaves, and fruit all derive their life and comeliness from their relation to the parent trunk. Jesus applied the law of radiation to the art of living when He said to His disciples, "I am the vine, ye are the branches,"[44] while Paul utilized the same principle by referring to the Church as the body of which Christ is the head.[45]

6. The Law of Contrast. The law of association by comparison and contrast is so obvious in all the arts that comment upon it might seem at first unnecessary. According to Ruskin, Turner hardly ever "allows a strong light to oppose a full dark, without some intervening tint. His suns never set behind dark mountains without a film of cloud above the mountain's edge." In Biblical composition the range of association utilized to achieve unity runs through all its degrees from sharp antithesis to mild comparison. For this reason the reading of the Bible requires more than ordinary discrimination. And Ruskin's wise counsel may well be heeded. If all lines "were equally weighty, there would be no real sense of weight anywhere; if all were equally melodious, the melody itself would be fatiguing." When the reader correctly observes the degree of contrast indicated in a statement, he is enabled to judge for himself where the author's emphasis really lies. Contrast reveals differences which might not otherwise be obvious, or it exhibits dissimilar qualities in things which are compared. Jesus employed contrast effectively in His teaching. This is well illustrated in the Sermon on the Mount, where He used contrast in imagery: light and darkness, white and black, and the two houses. He differentiated between the new and the old

orders of life in His repeated formula, "Ye have heard that it was said to them of old time . . . but I say unto you." He set true and false practices over against each other as related to giving, praying, and fasting. He developed His exposition in terms of opposed ideas like kinds of righteousness and types of treasure. He gave clues to other contrasts in His careful use of connectives like *but, or,* and *else,* and so on. His parables like the Prodigal Son, the Good Samaritan, and the Four Soils are based on the law of contrast. Likewise in the Old Testament, the reader recognizes how the use of striking contrasts illumines the Psalms (as for instance Psalm 1), and the Prophets (as for instance Isaiah 1).

These six most commonly used laws of arrangement—Principality, Repetition, Continuity, Curvature, Radiation, and Contrast—are among the most readily available instruments for opening the eyes of the understanding. Ruskin mentions three others: Interchange, Consistency, and Harmony. Interchange, closely connected with Contrast, "enforces the unity of opposite things, by giving to each a portion of the character of the other." Luke in his Gospel heightens the interest of the reader and adds to the significance of the birth of Jesus, by using this law effectively in his so-called Infancy Narrative. Following the Preface to his Gospel he develops the narrative by telling of the announcement of John's coming (1:5-25); then of the announcement of Jesus' coming (1:26-56); then of the birth of John (1:57-80); then of the birth of Jesus (2:1-21). Thus the unity of the narrative is not only enhanced, but the mutual relations and differences between John the Baptist and Jesus are strengthened and enforced. Consistency and Harmony are not so much laws of composition, as laws of truth. They are really the outcomes of the other laws. They are good tests by which the unity of a composition may be judged. They might well be stated in the form of questions: How advantageously has the author resolved the opposites in his composition? Are the several parts in the composition in balance, or out of proportion to each other? A reading of Ruskin's whole essay, which forms an appendix to this volume, will suggest other instructive aspects of these laws.

THE EDUCATION OF THE UNDERSTANDING

We have shown that sharpened senses and the power to understand are intimately connected. A growing ability to understand, whether viewed in terms of aesthetic response, or of scientific inquiry, or of the fulfillment of moral relations, involves alert and focused sense impressions. The laws of composition provide an objective guide to exact observation. By recognizing these laws of composition in Biblical passages which are familiar and appealing, and thus finding the sources of their power, the student educates his eye to trace the more disguised patterns in a strange or unfamiliar medium. Let him start with his Bible where he knows it best, and ere he is aware he will be lured into wider reading, or he will be encouraged to undertake more difficult passages. Habits of exact observation and patient comparison will lead to accurate judgment. These processes will mutually assist in opening the eyes of the understanding.

N O T E S

The quotations on the title page of this chapter are from *The Glory of the Imperfect,* by George Herbert Palmer, pp. 63, 64, and from *The Journal of Henry David Thoreau,* November 1, 1851.

1. Matthew 13:13.
2. Luke 8:18. See Luke 6:27, 47, 49; 8:8, 21.
3. See Luke 7:18-23.
4. See Lane Cooper, *Louis Agassiz as a Teacher,* p. 1. Comstock Publishing Co., Ithaca, New York, 1945.
5. "Blind," in *Chanteys and Ballads,* by Harry Hibbard Kemp, p. 119. Brentano's, New York, 1920. Reproduced by permission of the author.
6. Richard Guggenheimer, *Sight and Insight,* Preface, pp. vii, viii. Harper & Brothers, New York, 1945. Quoted by permission of the publisher.
7. Robert Louis Stevenson, *Virginibus Puerisque* (Thistle Edition), Vol. 13, Chapter IV. "Truth of Intercourse," p. 48. He refers at this place to Thoreau, *A Week on the Concord and Merrimack Rivers,* Wednesday, p. 283.
8. S. T. Coleridge, *Aids to Reflection,* Preface, pp. 63, 65. Chauncy Goodrich, Burlington, Vermont, 1840.

9. Psalm 119:130. See Jeremiah 26:10; Ezekiel 41:11. Delitzsch, *Biblical Commentary on the Psalms* (Second Edition), Vol. III, p. 259, comments, "The opening, the disclosure of God's word giveth light, inasmuch as it makes the simple wise or sagacious."

10. Coleridge, *op. cit.*, p. 217, 218.

11. John Oman, *Vision and Authority*, Revised Edition, p. 46. Harper and Brothers, New York, 1929.

12. *The Bulletin*, Metropolitan Museum of Art, New York, December, 1944. Vol. III, No. 4. Article, "But It's Not a Cimabue!" by William S. Ivins, Jr., p. 100. Used by permission of the publisher.

13. Theodore Meyer Greene, *The Arts and the Art of Criticism*, p. 16.

14. P. W. Bridgman, *The Logic of Modern Physics*. See pp. 39-45. Macmillan Co., New York, 1927.

15. *Ibid.*, p. 42. This quotation (and the above) is used by permission of the publisher.

16. Tract *Aboth*, Chapter 2, Mishna 7, *The Babylonian Talmud*, Edited by I. Epstein. The Soncino Press, London, 1935.

17. John 5:39, 40.

18. Jeremiah 23:18, 22.

19. Mark 7:8-13.

20. Matthew 6:21-23.

21. Luke 8:16-18.

22. See Calvin, *Institutes of the Christian Religion*, Book I, Chapters 6 and 7. Translated by John Allen, Vol. I, pp. 72, 79, 80. Presbyterian Board of Publication, Philadelphia, 1909.

23. John 16:13.

24. Richard Guggenheimer, *op. cit.*, p. viii.

25. George Moore, *Héloïse and Abélard*, in two volumes, Vol. I, p. 42. Boni and Liveright, New York, 1921. Used by permission of Liveright Publishing Corporation.

26. *Ibid.*, Vol. I, p. 69.

27. *The Autobiography of Nathaniel Southgate Shaler*, pp. 98, 99. Houghton Mifflin Company, New York, 1909. Used by permission of copyright proprietor.

28. Samuel H. Scudder, "In the Laboratory with Agassiz," *Every Saturday*, April 4, 1874. No. 16, pp. 369, 370. See also Lane Cooper, *op. cit.*, for other essays on Agassiz's use of direct observation as the primary instrument of teaching.

29. *The Works of Ralph Waldo Emerson*, Four Volumes in One. Tudor Publishing Co., New York. Vol. 3, pp. 441, 442.

30. John Ruskin, *Modern Painters*, Vol. V. Second Edition, p. 48.

31. Theodore Meyer Greene, *op. cit.*, p. 372.

32. See H. R. Poore, *Pictorial Composition*, G. P. Putnam's Sons, New York, 16th Impression, p. 13; and Dudley and Faricy, *The Humanities*, p. 7.

33. Theodore Meyer Greene, *op. cit.*, p. 14.

34. At this point the reader may find it desirable to consult the abridged version of Ruskin's *Essay on Composition* which forms the Appendix of this volume.

35. H. R. Poore, *op. cit.*, p. 13.

36. Mark 4:31-33; Matthew 13:31, 32; Luke 13:18, 19.

37. Isaiah 9:8—10:4.

38. Jeremiah 3:1—4:2.

39. Matthew 5:21, 22; 27, 28; 31, 32; 33, 34; 38, 39; 43, 44.

40. Revelation 2:7, 11, 17, 29; 3:6, 13, 22.

41. Luke 4:14-30.

42. Luke 5:17—6:11.

43. *Cf.* Luke 8:19-21 and Mark 3:31-35.

44. John 15:5.

45. Ephesians 1:22, 23; 5:23.

THE FORM AND POWER OF HOLY SCRIPTURE

"Form is apt to be a more permanent pre-servative for a book than substance."
                    —Ellery Sedgwick.

"The bricklayer theory [of learning] exalts the virtue of collecting factual bricks; but it neglects the primary virtue of drawing structural plans. It understands the function of bricklaying better than the function of architecture . . . We have been painstaking in pursuit of detail but conventional or frivolous in the harder intellectual labor of thought."—Thomas Clark Pollock.

F O U R

The Form and Power of Holy Scripture

DEFINITION OF FORM

As a bearer of true light Holy Scripture comes to men in the familiar literary forms of history and poetry, proverb and parable, discourse, meditation, and apocalypse. For this reason Scripture takes its place among the arts as literature. Like all the arts, therefore, it may be viewed in terms of the three commonly recognized basic categories which assist the sensitive observer to explore any work, namely: matter, form, and content.

According to definition, the *matter* of a work of art is that in it which has been expressively organized. Its *form* is the expressive organization of its matter. Its *content* is that which finds expression through such formal organization.[1] These categories may be applied to the New Testament, for instance, as follows: In our New Testament there are four Gospels: Matthew, Mark, Luke, and John. The subject matter of each is the same—the life and teachings of Jesus Christ. But the expressed content of each Gospel differs in scope and detail, the content in each case being determined by what was selected from the total subject matter available by each evangelist. The form of each Gospel is the manner in which this available subject matter is expressively organized.

Now it is obvious that what determines the distinctive merit of any work is not what it says but how it says it, not its expressed content but its expressive form. By distinctive merit observe that we are not referring to its value as truth but rather to its impact as a mode of expression upon the observer. The same truth uttered by different individuals makes a different impact upon the hearer by virtue

• 91 •

of the manner in which it is expressed. Also, a single individual may say the same thing more cogently upon one occasion than upon another. Thomas Babington Macaulay illustrates this in his reference to Samuel Johnson's literary prose.[2] He tells us that Johnson, while on his journey to the Hebrides, wrote a personal letter to his friend Mrs. Thrale in which he said: "When we were taken upstairs a dirty fellow bounced out of the bed on which one of us was to lie." This incident when later published in the record of his "Journey" appeared as follows: "Out of one of the beds on which we were to repose, started up, at our entrance, a man as black as a Cyclops from the forge." Upon another occasion when referring to the comedy entitled, "The Rehearsal," Johnson is reported to have said: "It has not wit enough to keep it sweet"; then after a pause, "It has not vitality enough to preserve it from putrefaction." Form does give quality to the effective power of an utterance, and to recognize form is to open up a direct avenue to the sources of its power. To exalt form as an end in itself, however, as is sometimes done, is to stifle the very purpose for which expression in any form exists.

That F. W. Robertson understood the importance of form is indicated by his letter of reassurance to a confused friend in which he said, "I am blind and ignorant but I can see this at least, that the blue, red, yellow, etc., reflected from the sky, and bush, and sea, are not the light itself, but only reflected fragments of the light; the 'elements of the world' on which the light is broken, but yet made visible. Some day you will feel this."[3] He might well have said, "You must feel this," for form is that element in a literature in which the light of its subject matter is made visible. Form likewise gives a distinctive quality to its expressed content. We are making no attempt here to discuss the comparative merit of these three categories in relation to each other. We are merely seeking to emphasize the importance of form as a tool of intelligent understanding. Form is the key which unlocks the door of content and discloses the essence of subject matter. Form plays a functional role in recreative method by awakening and training the understanding.

THE IMPORTANCE OF FORM

To become form-conscious is essential in anyone's general education. It would hardly be too much to say that the failure to awaken
and train this type of conscious awareness is a direct cause of the
chronic complaint that American children cannot read, write, or
speak their own language properly. But this is not an American ailment only. In 1943, His Majesty's Stationery Office in Great Britain
published the report of the Norwood Committee on *Curriculum and
Examinations in Secondary Schools.*[4] This committee, reporting on
evidence gleaned from "Universities, professional bodies, firms and
business houses, training colleges, and many other interests and
many individuals," summarized its findings by saying: "The complaint briefly is that too many pupils show marked inability to present ideas clearly to themselves, to arrange them, and to express them
clearly on paper or in speech; they read without sure grasp of what
they read, and they are too often at a loss in communicating what
they wish to communicate in clear and simple sentences and in expressive and audible tone." This ailment is certainly more elemental
than mere inability to read. It is clearly a functional lack in the art
of understanding as well as in the art of self-expression: a defect in
consciousness of form.

The above report on British secondary education is paralleled by
that of a committee appointed by the American Council on Education, entitled *Reading in General Education,* 1940. This committee, which enlarged its inquiry to include adult education, found
that "an appalling number of our adult population . . . read with
difficulty, with poor understanding, and with little enjoyment."[5]
One investigator who lays this lack to the character of language
teaching in our schools declares, "At the moment, the teacher of
language is little better than a medicine man, practicing charms
taught him by his ancestors upon an ailment which he but dimly
understands."[6] Whatever truth there may be in this assertion the

ailment nevertheless remains chronic. It is one of the inevitable outcomes of a general educative process which emphasizes facts and items of knowledge without cultivating a corresponding ability to see things in their true relations. In raising up a generation intent upon content we have left it blind to form. This failure of general education is doubtless responsible for a corresponding defect in Christian education. But this does not mean that we must wait for it to be remedied by the schools. No more perfect exemplar exists for illustrating the significance of form and its use as a tool in educating the understanding than the Holy Scriptures themselves. In considering the form and power of Scripture we may ask how this weakness may be corrected.

Becoming Form-Minded

No one has described the process of becoming form-minded better than John Ruskin in his appeal for a "recovery of what may be called *the innocence of the eye* . . . as a blind man would see if suddenly gifted with sight."[7] For instance, Ruskin says, "When grass is lighted strongly by the sun in certain directions it is turned from green into a peculiar and somewhat dusty-looking yellow. If we had been born blind, and were suddenly endowed with sight on a piece of grass thus lighted in some parts by the sun, it would appear to us that part of the grass was green, and part a dusty yellow (very nearly of the colour of primroses); and, if there were primroses near, we should think that the sunlighted grass was another mass of plants of the same sulphur-yellow colour. We should try to gather some of them, and find that the colour went away from the grass when we stood between it and the sun, but not from the primroses; but by a series of experiments we should find out that the sun was really the cause of the colour in the one,—not in the other. We go through such processes of experiment unconsciously in childhood; and having once come to conclusions touching the significance of certain colours, we always suppose that we *see* what we only know, and have hardly any consciousness of the real aspect of the signs we have learned to interpret. Very few people have any idea that sun-lighted grass is yellow."[8]

How then does anyone become conscious of the real aspect of the signs of knowledge he is called upon to interpret and how may he use this ability when he opens the Scriptures? The first step in this direction is to recognize the relation between matter, form, and con-tent. The content of our sixty-six books of Holy Scripture is as varied as the interests and needs of men. In this sense the content of Scripture qualifies as a true mirror of life. "The men and women of the Old Testament—their sensations, emotions, ideas—are ex-actly the same as ours at the present day. On the side of giving a mirror to life and all varieties of living, the Old Testament," accord-ing to Duncan Black Macdonald, "is more modern than all the New except the words of Christ Himself."[9] But merely to stop with the expressed content of Scripture, however valuable such knowl-edge is, would be to miss the very thing for which it exists as the vehicle of communicating a vital subject matter. The essence of this subject matter is its power-giving quality.

What Paul Meant by Form

Let us allow the Apostle Paul to define this for us. In his Epistle to the Romans (2:17ff), Paul addresses the Jew as one who rests upon the law and glories in God. Paul uses the word law in a variety of ways, but it is clear that when he speaks of *law* here (νόμῳ 2:17) he means the revealed will of God disclosed in the Hebrew Scriptures. He indicates that the Jew is one who takes pride in his distinction as a teacher of others and suggests that the Jew has "in the law the form of knowledge and of the truth."[10] In other words, according to Paul, the Jew had in the expressed content of the Old Testament the form of knowledge and truth which me-diated to him the revealed will of God, i.e., the expressed subject mat-ter of his Scriptures. While Paul did not speak of these three cate-gories of literary expression as such he recognized, nevertheless, their distinctive functions in mediating the knowledge of God found in the Hebrew Scriptures.

What did Paul mean by the expression "the *form* of knowledge and of the truth"? The word he uses here for form is *morphōsis*. Like its corresponding substantive *morphē, morphōsis* refers originally, as Lightfoot has shown, to the organs of sense. *"Morphē* comprises all those sensible qualities, which striking the eye lead to the conviction that we see such and such a thing." In other words, whatever we can see, feel, or hear is the form of a material object. In a similar manner, whatever we can conceive is the form of a mental object. Anything which is to enter within the range of an individual's cognition (Kant called it *das Ding an sich,* the thing itself) must become a phenomenon. Its *morphē* is its mode of entering into the individual's cognition. Its *morphōsis* is the act of making itself known or the mode of its continued existence. Olin A. Curtis offers this simple illustration: "The *morphē* of a mountain ash is the entire combination of essential characteristics which are necessary to constitute and manifest that individual thing we call a mountain ash. Take away even one of these characteristics and it would not be a mountain ash . . . Thus, the *morphē* of the tree is the tree's typical or mountain ash individuality."[11] The *morphōsis* of that tree is the actual process of its entering into my personal knowledge as a distinct entity called mountain ash.

To paraphrase Paul, *morphōsis* (form) is the embodiment of that particular knowledge and truth of divine revelation (subject matter) which is expressed in that part of Holy Scripture called the Old Testament (content).[12] Form mediates the vital subject matter of Holy Scripture in its expressed content.

When once a given subject matter has taken shape in an expressed content three pertinent questions may be asked about it: First, when and by whom was this composed? This is the historical question. Second, what is here (content), and how is it expressed (form)? This is the re-creative question. Third, of what value is the composition? This is the judicial question. These three questions (as we have shown elsewhere, p. 58), are intimately related to each other and are not mutually exclusive. Let us consider at this point the historian's use of form and the re-creative use of form.

THE HISTORIAN'S USE OF FORM

When form is used as a tool by the literary historian in the study of origins the technical term is form criticism. For two and a half decades this type of study has been applied with rigor to the study of Gospel origins. Utilizing form as a tool, such historians have sought to determine what clues our written Gospels furnish as to their pre-literary stage when the units of Gospel tradition were taking shape and were transmitted orally. The beginnings of this method of New Testament study were made by Martin Dibelius in 1919 in his treatise, *Die Formgeschichte des Evangeliums.*[13] Other German scholars employing this method were K. L. Schmidt, Rudolf Bultmann, and Martin Albertz. In England, R. H. Lightfoot, Vincent Taylor, and E. Basil Redlich; and in America, B. S. Easton, F. C. Grant, D. W. Riddle, and others have led in this type of study. Dibelius began with two basic considerations. The first of these was that the authors of our Gospels were mainly collectors or editors. They did not originate materials but merely organized reported sayings of Jesus, or stories told about Him, into a chronological and geographical framework and thus produced our Gospels. The second was that the materials they used already existed in a certain Gestaltung (formation) which was determined by the definite needs of early Christians. Certain units of expression in the tradition about Jesus took shape in direct relation to the "life situation" (*Sitz im Leben*) of the Christian community. For this reason, Dibelius argued, a knowledge of the requirements and interests of the primitive church should enable us to detect the modifications through which the individual structural units of the Gospels have passed.

The methods and results of form criticism are now quite well known in the extensive literature available on the subject. We can pause here only to speak of form criticism as an illustration of the historical method. The historian using form criticism lifts a given passage out of its context in composition and classifies it according to type of traditional material. Different tags are used by the various critics, but typical units of tradition are identified as: the miracle story, the paradigm, the parable, the proverb, the apocalyptic saying, the passion story, etc. These types of material once identified by their characteristics are then related to their appropriate sequence in historical development. Thus the historian seeks to determine the laws of oral tradition and to evaluate the trustworthiness of our knowledge of the life of Jesus.

Among the positive contributions of form criticism four may be mentioned. First is the emphasis which has been placed upon the practical evangelistic importance to the early Church of the material out of which our Gospels were composed. Second, form criticism has shown that at one time much of this material existed in the form of separate units. Third, this type of historical study has also indicated how some of these units were combined for purposes of topical presentation, as for instance, Mark 2:1—3:6. Fourth, form criticism likewise has thrown light upon the practical problems faced by the primitive Church and has linked critical study with vital issues in early Church history. However, form criticism has its limitations. It cannot transcend the evidence provided by its categories of reference. It cannot account, for instance, for the primitive Church itself which gathered and selected the materials of the Gospels. This is to be found, as E. P. Dickie has shown, in the testimony, "not of historians, but in the histories of souls. The real presence of the Jesus of History is established by the experience of the Christian community, the Church down the ages and the Church today . . . and . . . by that which He has said to *us* and done for *us*."[14] The final evidence for the genuineness and authority of our Gospels as historic documents comes to us in the re-creation of Scripture by the Church itself. One direct, personal, and essential mode of re-creation is the use of form.

THE RE-CREATIVE USE OF FORM

Form criticism, since it is a highly specialized mode of study, can be used successfully only by an expert. The results of his work are then made available for the enlightenment and use of the common man. But re-creative use of form is available to anyone who will use his own native powers of observation guided by the laws of composition. This can be done by using an English version of Scripture, although ability to use the Greek or Hebrew original will be a most valuable resource. In order to specialize in Biblical studies such use of original languages is an imperative resource.

The form of any piece of composition is determined by its "structural ingredients." Every object of nature and every work of man consists of parts or units organically related to each other.[15] Like all other composition Holy Scripture has such structural ingredients. They are twofold: units of material and relations between units. To identify what is meant by units let us seek a clear definition of structure. We may define it in two ways: first, "Certain parts or features" of any composition "which are essential or necessary to its existence, as distinguished from those that are removable, detachable, etc. (as in Gothic architecture the pointed arch is part of the structure, and is not a decorative addition)"; second, "The parts or features that reveal the underlying design as opposed to those that complete the work or bring it into fullness of being."[16] Such parts or features not structural in character, which complete a work, are called texture. John Crowe Ransom offers the following illustration: "The walls of my room are obviously structural; the beams and boards have a function; so does the plaster, which is the visible aspect of the final wall. The plaster might have remained naked, aspiring to no character, and purely functional. But actually it has been painted, receiving color; or it has been papered, receiving color and design, though these have no structural value; and perhaps it has been hung with tapestry, or with paintings, for 'decoration.' The paint, the paper, the tapestry, are texture. It is logically unrelated to structure." That is, those parts which are vitally related to a thing's organized existence are structural; those parts which are not so related, but which may be detached or are decorative, are texture. Mr. Ransom now applies this distinction to literature. "A poem," says he, "is logical structure, having local texture . . . The intent of the good critic (or re-creative reader) becomes therefore to examine and define the poem with respect to its structure and its texture."[17]

STAGES IN THE RE-CREATIVE PROCESS

We now have in the recognition of form a valid mode of procedure for re-creating Scripture. Here is a consciously guided process which takes advantage of obvious structural features in the form of Scripture to unfold its individuality and release its power. Three stages are involved in this process: first, discovering compositional units; second, identifying relations between units; third, recognizing characteristic features which reveal underlying design.

Discovering Compositional Units

Our Bible lies before us in two great parts: the Old Testament and the New Testament. The Hebrew Bible has three parts: the Law (Torah), the Prophets (Earlier and Later), and the Writings, a total of 39 books. The New Testament is a composite of 27 books consisting of the Gospels, the Acts, the Epistles, and the Apocalypse. Other groupings are also recognizable. But let us go one step further. Each book or document is a composite also of parts. And here lies a difficulty. Our versions have been artificially divided into chapters and verses.

The chapter divisions as we find them in our English New Testament are probably the work of Stephen Langton in A.D. 1228.[18] He made these divisions first in the Latin Vulgate to make it easier to refer to the text. Subsequently they were applied also to the printed Greek New Testament and so found their way into the English versions. Any careful reader of both Old and New Testaments can recognize that chapter divisions do not always indicate true units of composition. The first chapter of the book of Genesis really ends at 2:3; the close of Exodus, chapter 5, actually is at 6:9; Deuteronomy, chapter 4, is a true unit through verse 40 but at verse 41 a new unit of composition begins; Isaiah, chapter 4, really begins at 4:2; Jeremiah's message against the prophets begins at 23:9; and so on. Similar artificiality is found in the New Testament chapter divisions, as for instance, Mark 2 really closes at 3:6; Luke 20 continues through 21:4; John 3 properly begins at 2.23; Romans 3 ends at verse 20; and so on.

The verse divisions in our Bible were apparently meant to be sense clauses, but often they obliterate rather than reveal the sense. This division of the text into verses, so we are told, was made by Robert Stephanus in 1551 while traveling on horseback from Paris to Lyons, which may account for some of the odd combinations which mar it.[19] It follows that one of the first steps in Biblical interpretation is to ignore chapter and verse divisions. Some more effective method of identifying parts in Biblical composition is therefore necessary if a serious reader is to utilize recognizable units as a basis of his growing understanding. Here literary form is a direct aid to the discovery of units, and it will be profitable now to indicate how units of expression may be identified in Biblical composition.

Identifying Units of Expression

The basic element in all communication is the word or, to be more precise, the term. (Words may have many meanings, a term can have only one meaning at any given place.) The next most basic unit of expression is the sentence. A good sentence is the particular combination of words which expresses one single idea. A grouping of sentences which forms a unit of expression is called a paragraph. Because of its arrangement into paragraph units the excellence of the American Standard Version of the Bible as a study text cannot be too highly emphasized. Critical examination of this paragraph arrangement indicates an achievement of extraordinary excellence. Occasionally close scrutiny reveals that the revisers did not punctuate the text correctly and some more exact identification for the serious student is desirable. But on the whole the re-creative reader will find the paragraph divisions of the American Standard Version a reliable guide to the identification of units. The paragraph units of the Revised Standard Version of the New Testament (1946), on the whole, are an improvement of the text.

It is to be recognized, of course, that such paragraph division of the text is purely editorial. There are no such specific paragraph divisions in the oldest manuscripts nor, so far as we know, in the autographs. All that can be affirmed is that any object of nature or any work of man which has any worth or excellence at all takes shape only by recognizable articulation of units or parts, and it is the problem of the observer, by whatever means, correctly to detect and identify these parts. Paragraph indentation makes these parts more readily observable. This is no less important in the process of firsthand acquaintance with Scripture than it is in understanding the functional character of any piece of work.

We have now recognized three possible units of expression, the word, the sentence, the paragraph. It is obvious that sometimes two, three, four, or more paragraphs are connected in a recognizable unity by some idea, topic, or combination of relations. To identify such a grouping of paragraphs some descriptive term other than chapter is necessary. A convenient identifying term is *segment*, for such a grouping sometimes may be part of a chapter or of several chapters. By definition, the term segment "is often preferred to section for a part cut off by natural lines of cleavage or necessitated by the nature of the thing's construction or design; as, a *segment* of an orange, a *segment* of a compound leaf; a *segment* of a flywheel; the *segment* of the globe known as the Torrid Zone."[20] So a *segment* of Scripture is any grouping of paragraphs which forms a single observable unity. This unity may be loose or it may be very closely articulated. In any case the problem of the individual observer is to recognize what marks of unity are present and to discover in what manner the paragraphs which compose this unity are related to each other. These relations are the most readily available firsthand marks of the composer's intentions. Finally, to recognize a grouping of segments in a book the term *section* may be employed.

We may now summarize what we have said and enumerate the types of compositional units which await the exploring eye of the observer. By proceeding from the whole to the parts in any document or book we may recognize at least five types of unit: the section, the segment, the paragraph, the sentence, and the word. In larger and more complex books it may be necessary to employ still further nomenclature for recognizable units, such as *portion* to designate a grouping of segments within a section, or *division* for a grouping of sections. But whatever terminology may be devised, the first step in any serious firsthand acquaintance with a book of Scripture, apart from general reading, is to discover units and to identify them.

Two modes of procedure are possible. The one is structural, the other is interpretative. Structural or analytical attention proceeds from a given whole to its parts. Interpretative or synthetic attention proceeds from the parts to a given whole. In practical experience the resolving of a whole into its parts normally precedes that of composing or recomposing parts into an organized whole. It is both desirable and necessary to keep in mind that the two processes do not involve different kinds of attention but only a different order in performance. Since any given whole is greater than its parts and cannot function without them, it follows that structural attention should precede interpretative attention. Analysis should always precede synthesis. "Image the whole," said Robert Browning, "then execute the parts."[21]

When structural attention is given to the Bible we may work in the large in order to gain perspective and so proceed from a whole book to the discovery of its sections. In the book of Exodus, for

instance, the sections are clearly recognizable by virtue of the geographical distribution of the parts: Chapters 1-12 in Egypt; 13-18
on the way to Sinai; 19-40 at Sinai. Closer study will reveal still
other marks of unity within these sections. Similarly in the Synoptic Gospels the Galilean ministry of Jesus is readily identified as a
section by geographical references, Mark 1:14—9:50 corresponding to Matthew 4:12—18:35 and to Luke 4:14—9:50. In other
books where exposition rather than narrative is the dominant type
of composition, sections are readily detected by the treatment of
ideas or subjects, as for instance in the Epistle to the Romans; or by
personal, doctrinal, and practical aspects of a single theme, as in the
Epistle to the Galatians. In Philippians, however, such clear sec-
tional organization is not as apparent for it is a letter composed upon
considerations of "feeling and of memory, not of logic."[22]

A more convenient compositional unit for study purposes is the
segment. A segment represents a grouping of paragraphs which
forms a unity within a limited scope of treatment. The Gospel according to Luke is the most artistically arranged of our four Gospels and deserves Renan's encomium, "The most beautiful book
ever written." Chapters 1 through 9 (properly 1 through 9:50) are
a masterpiece of organizational unity. Here chapter and verse divisions are very misleading and have value only by way of convenience
of reference. But a clear impression of structural relations may be
discerned readily when the paragraph divisions of the text are utilized to full advantage. Luke was a master of the transitional sentence, a device which gives a mark of finish to his work. By print-
ing these transitional sentences as independent sentence-paragraphs
our revisers have made it possible for even the most inexperienced
reader to detect in most cases where Lukan segments begin and end.
The reader observes, for instance, how the so-called Infancy Narrative following the Preface is organized into segments: the annunciation of John (3 paragraphs); the annunciation of Jesus (3 paragraphs); the birth and naming of John (3 paragraphs); the birth
and naming of Jesus (3 paragraphs). In a similar manner he ob-

serves how the visit of Jesus to the temple (2 paragraphs); the ministry of John the Baptist (5 paragraphs); the genealogy of Jesus (1 paragraph); and the temptation of Jesus (2 paragraphs) are segments, each of which presents a different center of interest in Luke's narrative. Yet these four clearly recognizable parts conspire together to form one single unity in delineating the Sonship of Jesus. So, too, the Sabbath incident in the synagogue of Nazareth (2 paragraphs); the popular acclaim of Jesus by the multitudes (7 paragraphs); and the mounting opposition of the Pharisees and scribes (6 paragraphs) all are organized segments, and each is arranged in a climactic order.

The paragraph is also a compositional unit. A good paragraph in any composition is the effective treatment of a single topic or item of interest by means of properly arranged sentences. The mechanics of our modern English versions of Scripture cannot be too highly praised. By subordinating the old verse divisions and by presenting the text in paragraph divisions instead, our translators have rendered an inestimable service to firsthand observation. Occasionally their judgment concerning a paragraph may be questioned, but this is to be found usually in a passage where unity is either very loose or obscure.

Recognizing Characteristic Features

In paragraph study Ruskin's laws of composition operate effectively in assisting the reader to detect not only what degree of unity exists within the paragraph but also to observe the characteristic features of the author's treatment. These features are revealed in his choice of words, phrasing, imagery, and other marks of texture. The essential qualities of the author's treatment now begin to lay hold upon his mind, to enliven his imagination, to evoke intelligent understanding, and to awaken an appraising response.

By the time the reader has reached the sentence and the word, which are the basic elements of communication, he is ready to make the transition to the interpretative stage of his study by observing the relation of part to part. When attention is concentrated upon the word and upon the sentence, progress sometimes seems to be retarded, but in effect it is now greatly enhanced since it has been preceded by acquaintance in broader relations. At this stage the student finds recourse to a variety of aids both desirable and necessary. These various aids correspond to different kinds of problems which are raised in serious study. For help in determining the meaning of words he turns to the lexicon. In matters of syntax—the process of analyzing and classifying the modes of expression presented by a language—he turns to the grammar. To follow up the broader usage of words he will consult the concordance. The Bible Dictionary will provide him with general information relating to topics, facts, and questions of research in history, geography, philology, and pronunciation. The Atlas will enable him to orient his work in terms of the map. Commentaries on the various books will offer him assistance in matters of introduction, exegesis, or finished exposition. Ability to read the text in the original languages will be indispensable if he is to specialize in Biblical studies.

In our exposition up to this point we have stressed the structural order of study not only because it normally precedes the interpretative order but because its importance as a phase of the learning process has been comparatively neglected in the teaching of the Bible. By giving structural attention to a book, let us emphasize again, we work within recognizable units from a given whole to its parts. This process of discovering and identifying parts might seem at first, to the serious student, to be too elementary. Actually it is fully as essential as recognizing and identifying the parts of the human body are to the study of anatomy. For to recognize parts and their functions in relation to each other is necessary for firsthand understanding of any object. Although in the study of anatomy there still is much confusion in nomenclature for identifying parts, due to "an attempt to revise and improve the terminology which had previously been in common use,"[23] no physician would be considered competent who was unable to differentiate in some way the several parts and their functions. What we are attempting to emphasize just now is the fact that in our American Standard Version of the Bible (or in the Revised Standard Version of the New Testament) we have a text which makes it possible to begin and to advance this process of firsthand acquaintance so essential to intelligent understanding and enjoyment of Scripture.

FORM AS AN INSTRUMENT TO RELEASE POWER

So far our study has attempted to show that form not only unfolds the meaning of subject matter but also serves as an effective instrument for the release of power.

One of the leading American literary figures of the past generation was Gamaliel Bradford, who specialized in the writing of biographies. Because he organized his portraits of character around a psychological pattern he referred to his works as psychographs. He was so successful in developing this type of presentation that his name has come to be identified with it in biographical writing. His method of treatment has been described as twofold. First, the continual stressing of the most recognizable dominant traits in a subject. Second, the relating of these traits to their corresponding motives. By this method Mr. Bradford succeeded "in making known qualities vibrant" and gave them an intensity that made them seem no longer mere platitudes of character. But one valid criticism of Mr. Bradford's work reveals his essential weakness in communicating truth. His interest in portraiture was so intense that he neglected the ideas which animated the characters he portrayed. One of Mr. Bradford's most able critics has analyzed this weakness as follows: "He portrayed men in their expression, in action, and in the effect they had on other people . . . but of the ideas which animated them he was mainly uncritical. He seldom made a judgment upon them of any sort." The result is that his work has "no core."[24]

This criticism of Mr. Bradford's psychographs indicates one of the limitations of secular literature. The lack of an adequate core, so characteristic of modern literary effort, throws into clear relief the essential nature of Scripture. It is "a type of utterance which comes from a center different from that from which the corrupted mortal is speaking . . . It is not aspiring upwards, but bringing the light downwards to earth."[25] It has a core of reality with which men must reckon. Its power-giving character, mediated through the instrumentality of form, is uncompromising in its claim upon the whole man. It not only portrays life, it requires life. However, we may profitably make use of Mr. Bradford's method of making "known qualities vibrant." Form mediates "the most recognizable dominant traits" in an expressed content. Form enables us to see how these traits are related to their corresponding motives. Form releases what is vital in the subject matter of Scripture.

NOTES

The first quotation on the title page of this chapter is from *The Atlantic Monthly*, July, 1946, p. 69; and the second is from Thomas Clark Pollock, *The Nature of Literature*, p. xvii, published by the Princeton University Press.

1. See Theodore Meyer Greene, *The Arts and the Art of Criticism*, pp. 31, 32.
2. In Macaulay's Essay on Croker's Edition of Boswell's *Life of Johnson* (Edinburgh Review, September, 1831). This is reproduced in Longmans' English Classics, edited by H. B. Buehler, p. 74. Longmans, Green and Co., New York, 1896.
3. *Life, Letters, Lectures, and Addresses of F. W. Robertson*, p. 258. Harper and Brothers, New York, 1865.
4. See *Curriculum and Examinations in Secondary Schools*. Report of the Committee of the (Great Britain) Secondary School Examinations Council Appointed by the President of the Board of Education in 1941, London, 1, His Majesty's Stationery Office, 1943, p. 13.
5. *Reading in General Education*. An Exploratory Study, Edited by William S. Gray. See Foreword, p. v. American Council on Education, Washington, D. C., 1940.
6. *Ibid.*, p. 112.
7. John Ruskin, *Elements of Drawing and Elements of Perspective*. Everyman's Library, 217; pp. 3, 4. E. P. Dutton and Co., New York.
8. *Ibid.*, p. 4.
9. Duncan Black Macdonald, *The Hebrew Literary Genius*, pp. xxi, xxii. Princeton University Press, 1933.
10. Romans 2:20.
11. Olin A. Curtis, *The Christian Faith*, p. 238.
12. In the Revised Standard Version of the New Testament (1946), the word *embodiment* is used to translate μόρφωσις, Romans 2:20.

13. This work by Martin Dibelius in its English edition is entitled *From Tradition to Gospel*, and was translated from the revised second edition, in collaboration with the author, by Bertram Lee Woolf. Ivor Nicholson and Watson, Ltd., London, 1934. Other typical works in English which describe or employ form criticism are, B. S. Easton, *The Gospel Before the Gospels*, Charles Scribner's Sons, New York, 1928; R. H. Lightfoot, *History and Interpretation in the Gospels*, The Bampton Lectures 1934, Hodder and Stoughton, London, 1935. The principles of form criticism are examined and evaluated by F. V. Filson, *One Lord, One Faith*, Westminster Press, Philadelphia, 1943, pp. 35-42; and Lawrence J. McGinley, *Form-criticism of the Synoptic Healing Narratives.* A study in the theories of Martin Dibelius and Rudolf Bultmann. Woodstock College Press, Woodstock, Maryland, 1944.

14. E. P. Dickie, *Revelation and Response*, p. 171.

15. See Greene, *The Arts and the Art of Criticism*, pp. 126, 127.

16. *Webster's Dictionary of Synonyms*, p. 797.

17. See Donald A. Stauffer, Editor, *The Intent of the Critic*, Princeton University Press, 1941, Essay, "Criticism as Pure Speculation," by John Crowe Ransom, pp. 110, 111.

18. Caspar René Gregory, *The Canon and Text of the New Testament*, p. 473. Charles Scribner's Sons, New York, 1907.

19. *Ibid.*, p. 474. Gregory thinks that the words "inter equitandum" may mean that Stephanus made his verse divisions between the stages of his trip.

20. *Webster's Dictionary of Synonyms*, p. 606.

21. Robert Browning, "A Grammarian's Funeral." Also see Adler, *How to Read a Book*, p. 124.

22. *A Commentary on the Holy Bible*, Edited by J. R. Dummelow, p. 968. The Macmillan Company, New York, 1917.

23. See article, Anatomy, in *The Encyclopedia Brittanica*, 14th edition, Vol. I, p. 880.

24. John Chamberlain, article, "Mr. Bradford Psychographs the Will to Power." New York *Times* Book Review, March 8, 1931, p. 5.

25. Lawrence Hyde, *The Prospects of Humanism*, pp. 162, 163.

SCRIPTURE AND FREEDOM TO THINK

*"Our vernacular Bible is a sign of our per-
sonal independence, our freedom from eccle-
siastical authority, our spiritual* MAGNA
CHARTA, *our Declaration of Rights. That
feeling did not exist in the Middle Ages."*
                    —John Alfred Faulkner.

*"A man can more easily burn down his own
house than get rid of his prejudices."*
                    —René Descartes.

FIVE

Scripture and Freedom to Think

&

AMONG THE CHARACTERISTICS of man, none are more distinctive than his native capacity to think and his passion to be free. In actual experience the passion to be free serves as an elemental drive to action, the capacity to think acts as a directing influence. Freedom to think thus constitutes at once man's most cherished gift and his most deadly peril. "The mind's eye," declares Victor Hugo, "can nowhere find anything more dazzling nor more dark than in man; it can fix itself upon nothing which is more awful, more complex, more mysterious, nor more infinite."[1] Man's power to pry into the secrets of the universe has enabled him to detect and smash the atom, and thus to unleash elemental forces. His freedom to think has brought him to the edge of the abyss. He is free to destroy himself or to rise to the true dignity for which he has been created.

No utterance of the prophets of Israel is more poignant in its appeal than the opening words of the prophecy of Isaiah: "Hear, O heavens, and give ear, O earth; for the Lord hath spoken: I have nourished and brought up children, and they have rebelled against me. The ox knoweth his owner, and the ass his master's crib; but Israel doth not know, my people doth not consider."[2] By these words Isaiah was not accusing his people of being ignorant. He bluntly charges them with abusing their freedom to think. Having dignified them as children of a divine Father, he contrasts men with brutes. A harnessed ox recognizes its owner and submits willingly to him; the ass knows whose hand it is that puts food into the manger. God's people display no such knowledge in their actions. Rather they are rebels. They bring neither instinct nor reflection to bear upon their relation to God, to whom they belong. They do not act as children of a nourishing Father upon whom they must depend for their very existence and prosperity. Israel doth not think! Insensitivity to the goodness of God had left its mark upon Isaiah's nation. Now he describes his people as "a seed of evil-doers, children that deal corruptly! . . . the whole head is sick, and the whole heart faint."[3]

THE FORMATIVE INFLUENCE OF IDEAS
UPON CHARACTER

The formative influence of ideas upon character was recognized by the wisdom of ancient Israel: "As a man thinketh in his heart, so is he."[4] Insensitivity to God's goodness had brought Isaiah's people to the verge of ruin. Upon the other hand, Scripture shows how the application of instinct and reflection to God's ways has a positive and healing influence. The Apostle Paul went to the heart of the matter when, in writing to a church torn by factions, he declared: "Finally, brethren, whatsoever things are true, whatsoever things are honorable, whatsoever things are just, whatsoever things are pure, whatsoever things are lovely, whatsoever things are of good report; if there be any virtue, and if there be any praise, think on these things." But Paul was not content to let the matter rest there. He added: "The things which ye both learned and received and heard and saw in me, these things do: and the God of peace shall be with you."[5] These are not the words of a boastful egoist. They are Paul's formula for verifying truth. What the Philippian Christians had learned from him they must put to the test of experience. He had embodied these virtues, about which he bids them think, in his own personal experience and so had demonstrated their validity. So must they. The power of ideas to influence man as a thinking person being admitted, it remains for a man to determine which ideas he will allow to influence him. Freedom to think and responsibility to choose between ideas therefore go hand in hand.

THE MEANING OF IDEAS

Our English word *idea* comes directly from the Greek ἰδέα (from the verb ἰδεῖν, to see). Plato used the word ἰδέα to express the look or semblance of a thing as opposed to reality. To him the ἰδέαι were general or ideal forms, that is, pattern forms, or archetype models, of which all created things were the imperfect antitypes or representations. These copies or representations have their being, according to Plato, only as they participate in the realities they represent.[6]

Since the sixteenth century, however, the word *idea* has been used to refer to any mental image or picture. Descartes, Locke, Berkeley, and Hume applied the term to any immediate object of thought, so that it might be used to identify anything that an individual feels when he feels, or whatever he fancies when he fancies, or what he thinks when he thinks.[7] Anything directly present in a person's cognitive consciousness, then, is an idea whether it is a mere supposition or a verified fact; whether it is a good or a practical opinion or merely a ridiculous suggestion. It follows that every human individual has ideas, and that these ideas may have a potent influence for good or ill upon his character.

A modern father, speaking of his son, declares, "My boy Eric, at the age of ten, has opinions on more subjects than you can imagine. Justifying these, he asks, 'Haven't I a right to my opinion?' But I reply, 'Why should you have an opinion? What work have you done on this subject to entitle you to one? How much experience have you had in this affair, so that you can have a reliable opinion about it?' "[8] This wise father recognizes that merely to have ideas is not enough. What kind of ideas are they? Why do you hold them? What influence have they upon your conduct? How far have you verified them in actual experience? It is only by such practical tests that ideas of real worth may be sifted from the worthless; the true from the false; and the good from the evil. Every human being has a responsibility to himself to use his freedom to think by cross-examining his own personal experience.

In our own generation we have witnessed how an ideology of racial superiority may capture the imagination of a whole people and galvanize a nation into fanatical and almost irresistible zeal. We have also seen that it is not enough merely to destroy the weapons and the armies such a nation may forge to impose its will upon other nations. Its ideology must be changed. Its bad ideas must be supplanted by good ones, and these disseminated down to the smallest village.

THE RELATION OF IDEAS TO FREEDOM

Merely to teach ideas, however, is not enough. For the ideas which influence men most are those to which they give their loyalty. And men's loyalties are determined by their affections and their wills. Here is the secret of human tragedy. Man is free to think, yet is in bondage—in bondage to himself. His freedom to think has not been matched by an emancipation of his affections and his will. Human history is in fact the arena of time in which potent ideas compete with each other for men's loyalties. Men, free to think, give their loyalties to ruling ideas which either enslave or truly liberate them.

"Human freedom," declared Woodrow Wilson, "consists in perfect adjustment of human interests and human activities and human energies . . . We say of a boat skimming the water with light foot, 'How free she runs,' when we mean, how perfectly she is adjusted to the force of the wind, how perfectly she obeys the great breath out of the heavens that fills her sails. Throw her head up into the wind and see how she will halt and stagger, how every sheet will shiver and her whole frame be shaken, how instantly she is 'in irons,' in the expressive phrase of the sea. She is free only when you have let her fall off again and have recovered once more her nice adjustment to the forces she must obey and cannot defy."[9]

This nice adjustment of human interests, and activities, and energies, at bottom involves man's intentions.

When we recognize this intimate relation between human freedom and the influence of man's intentions upon the exercise of that freedom, the true function of Holy Scripture as an instrument of effecting emancipation is clearly seen.

SCRIPTURE AND THE EXERCISE OF FREEDOM

As an interpretation of human history, the Bible presents a true picture of this conflict between man's freedom to think and his responsibility to choose the ideas to which he will give his loyalties. It is the very essence of the story of the Garden of Eden.[10] It is the story of Joseph and his testings in Egypt. When his ideas of purity were put to a test under seduction he declared, "How then can I do this great wickedness, and sin against God?"[11] It is the story of Moses and the Israelites in the wilderness, where their understanding of the redemption from bondage was overcome by their appetite for the fleshpots of Egypt.[12] It is the story of Elijah and his struggle with the prophets of Baal.[13] It is the story of Jeremiah's futile attempt to correct the error of his generation which had forsaken the fountain of living waters, and had hewed out cisterns, broken cisterns which could hold no water.[14] It is the story of Jesus and His encounter with the subtle legalism of the Pharisees.[15] It is the story of Paul and his Judaistic adversaries.[16] It is dramatically summarized in the tender words of the Revelation: "Behold, I stand at the door and knock: if any man hear my voice and open the door, I will come in to him, and will sup with him, and he with me."[17]

This expression from the Revelation, like many others in Scripture, sets into clear relief the appeal of Scripture to man to exercise his freedom to the highest advantage. Since men are what they are, no higher appeal to their nature can possibly be found than by creating in them a sense of conscious grateful debtorship—love's claim upon a grateful heart! It is for this reason that Jesus wisely called the great words of Moses the first commandment: "Hear, O Israel; The Lord our God, the Lord is one: and thou shalt love the Lord thy God with all thy heart, and with all thy soul, and with all thy mind, and with all thy strength. The second is this, Thou shalt love thy neighbor as thyself. There is none other commandment greater than these."[18]

Let us observe, then, how Scripture appeals to man to exercise his freedom to utmost advantage. The greatness of these commandments as stated by Jesus is to be seen both in the claim upon which they are based and in the type of response which they enjoin. Let us consider first the claim made and then the response enjoined.

The Claim Made

The claim which the great commandment makes upon men's loyalties lies in its expression of the unique covenant relation between God and His people.[19] This relation, according to the passage in Deuteronomy from which Jesus quoted, is based upon two facts. The first of these is the affirmation concerning the being and character of God Himself made known in the words of Deuteronomy 6:4. The text and margin of the American Standard version indicate four possible English translations of the Hebrew text. They are as follows: "Hear, O Israel, Jehovah our God is one Jehovah" (text). Or, "Jehovah our God, Jehovah is one." Or, "Jehovah is our God, Jehovah is one." Or, "Jehovah is our God, Jehovah alone." The modern Jewish version accepts the second of the four and translates: "Hear, O Israel, the Lord our God, the Lord is one." Thus translated, these words affirm the unity of Israel's God, declaring that in His essence He is indivisible. But these same words may be interpreted with a higher and fuller meaning, as suggested by the fourth translation: "Hear, O Israel, Jehovah is our God, the Lord alone." In this case the words assert the uniqueness of Israel's God. And this interpretation with its richer significance, as Driver suggests, does not exclude the first, with its emphasis upon the unity of God.[20] The ground of the appeal to Israel's loyalty, first of all then, is seen to be the glorious being and character of the one God, whose unique relation to Israel has been made manifest to the fathers historically in His acts. This revelation of the one God, who claims the entire devotion of Israel, gives the clue to Israel's permanence and greatness. In Deuteronomy it is rightly recognized that the only salt able to keep the national life from rotting is an advancing knowledge of this God and His ways.

But there is a second basis upon which this appeal to loyalty rests. It is seen to be the covenant which this gracious God had initiated and established with Israel and which He had pledged Himself to fulfill. "Hear therefore, O Israel, and observe to do it; that it may be well with thee, and that ye may increase mightily, as the Lord, the God of thy fathers, hath promised unto thee . . . "[21] The peril which these people of Israel faced, as they were about to enter into the good land to enjoy its fruits, was that they would forget their gracious Benefactor and devote their loyalties to less worthy ends. This great utterance describes Moses drawing for his people an incomparable picture of the bountiful, unearned prosperity which the God of their fathers proposed to give them. And he combines with this picture of unmerited blessing a solemn warning: "And it shall be, when the Lord thy God shall bring thee into the land which he sware unto thy fathers, to Abraham, to Isaac, and to Jacob . . . then beware."[22] Why beware? These people are to beware lest their loyalties be turned from this gracious God to the enjoyment of their merely material advantages: land, houses, cisterns, vineyards, olive trees. When they should possess a land of promise, great and goodly cities which they did not build, houses full of good things which they did not fill, hewn cisterns which they did not dig, vineyards and olive trees which they did not plant; when they should eat and be full—then let them beware! "Beware," declares this prophetic voice, "Beware lest thou forget the Lord, who brought thee forth out of the land of Egypt, out of the house of bondage." How more urgently could love's claims be made real? These claims to undivided loyalty are made upon a people who were the recipients of undeserved bounties: heirs of a gracious promise made to the fathers; a people redeemed from cruel bondage by an unparalleled historic deliverance; a nation now about to become the beneficiary of bountiful, unmerited, material blessings. These are the tokens upon which the claims of God to undivided loyalty rest: the dual claim of His own gracious being and of His character made known and sealed in the making of Israel a covenant people.

The Response Enjoined

Having considered the claim made, let us now observe the nature of the response enjoined. Israel was free indeed, but responsible to choose a way of life based upon the highest motive. Moses rightly urged his people to give undivided allegiance to the one true source of all their boons. To love God with all one's heart, and with all one's soul, and with all one's might, is equivalent in Hebrew psychology to offering Him the devotion of one's whole being, for the "heart" is recognized as the organ of the intellect, and the "soul" as the organ of the desires or affections.[23]

These words of Scripture, therefore, call for a comprehensive life attitude on the part of God's people consonant with the enjoyment of their freedom to think. They are to love God to the uttermost with both intellect and affections. This love is to find its outreach in practical life relations. "These words, which I command thee this day, shall be upon thy heart," that is, they shall engage not only thoughts and feelings but be wrought into active intention. And intention is to be realized in practice. "These words . . . upon thy heart!" And because upon thy heart, teach them diligently to thy children. Because these words are upon thy heart, talk of them in thy home and in the market place; at the close and at the opening of the day, and so on. The order of this relation between inward apprehension and experience on the one hand, and the outward expression of it upon the other hand, is both profound and significant. First, commitment to God and His ways, then teaching; first, wholehearted dedication to the service of God, then talking about Him. Only so would the words upon the heart find appropriate and telling expression upon their lips. The chief end of man, as the Westminster Divines expressed it, is to "glorify God, and to enjoy Him forever."[24] Among the means to this end are teaching and testimony. What God's people had first experienced within as real, by the assertion of wholehearted integrity, they were to make effective in their outward relations.

A second aspect of the nature of this wholehearted response enjoined in Deuteronomy 6 is explicitly illustrated in the temptation experience of Jesus when He quoted from this passage. When shown all the kingdoms of the world and the glories of them (in a moment of time) and promised by the tempter, "All these things will I give thee, if thou wilt fall down and worship me," Jesus answered, "It is written, Thou shalt worship the Lord thy God, and him only shalt thou serve."[25] Here He was quoting from Deuteronomy 6:13, which reads, "Thou shalt fear the Lord thy God; and him shalt thou serve, and shalt swear by his name." Instead of the Hebrew verb for *fear,* Jesus uses the Greek verb, *to worship.* By using this term *to worship* by way of interpreting the Hebrew word for *fear,* Jesus emphasized the reverential aspect of true filial fear; a fear which does not degrade men but uplifts them; a fear which is described in the Proverbs as "the beginning of wisdom."[26] Thus Jesus' experience emphasizes a second element in this comprehensive life attitude claimed from God's people which has such a direct bearing on their freedom to think: fear, reverential awe, the reverence of a child for its father; the deference of the creature for the creator.

But there is still another element in this life attitude taught in Deuteronomy 6 and explicitly affirmed in the personal experience of Jesus. It is found in the words of Deuteronomy 6:16, which words are also quoted by Jesus in His temptation experience. When urged to cast Himself from the pinnacle of the temple as a proof of His divine Sonship, in the confidence that God's angels would not suffer Him to be harmed, Jesus said, "It is written, Thou shalt not make trial of the Lord thy God."[27] And Deuteronomy adds, "as ye tempted him in Massah."[28] At Massah the Israelites had suffered from lack of water, and they strove with Moses, and murmured against God, saying, "Is the Lord among us or not?"[29] Their sin, according to Moses, was not that they complained about the lack of water but that they argued from its absence that God had failed them; that He was not among them; that He was indifferent to their needs. To put God to a test in a moment of crisis, by requiring Him to prove His love and His care and His presence by a miraculous deliverance, was regarded both by Moses and by Jesus as presumption. God's love, God's care, God's presence, they affirmed, are genuine and real and are not to be measured by the nature of outward circumstances either favorable or unfavorable. The true filial attitude on their part was to be expressed by keeping diligently the commandments of the Lord their God, and His testimonies, and His statutes, whatever the temper of their outward circumstances might be.[30]

But Jesus also recognized still a fourth element in this comprehensive life attitude connected so intimately with freedom to think. It is expressed in the reply to the question, "What commandment is the first of all?"[31] Having made answer, "Thou shalt love the Lord thy God with all thy heart, and with all thy soul, and with all thy mind, and with all thy strength," Jesus added (quoting from Leviticus 19:18), "Thou shalt love thy neighbor as thyself. There is none other commandment greater than these." It is clear, then, that in the mind of Jesus this commandment to love one's neighbor is meant to be co-ordinate with the commandment to love God, and that it springs from the same high motive: an obligation to fulfill personal relations within the covenant, both to God and to man. Thus Jesus interpreted the whole duty of man, drawing the elements of this comprehensive life attitude from its Old Testament setting: the unique character of the God of Israel and the historic manifestations of His faithfulness.

These called for a fourfold response from His people, a response consonant with their God-given freedom. First, the expression of wholehearted integrity—the law of love, first written on the heart, to be diligently taught and publicly asserted. Personal integrity is the heartthrob of freedom. Second, the maintaining of filial fear—reverential awe—for their Creator: the beginning of wisdom and the safeguard of freedom. Third, the bearing of a holy trust in God's unfailing goodness, faithfulness, and care, however tried or tested they might be by circumstance: the strength of freedom. Fourth, love for one's neighbor—a creative, energizing influence streaming from God's love for man, which inwardly prompts one to acts of love and deeds of mercy and kindness: the grace of freedom.

Since men's loyalties are determined by what they love, commitment to ideas and to causes is both crucial and decisive. It follows that a man's freedom to think is intimately and vitally connected with the kind of ideas and persons to which he commits himself. Let us give attention, then, to the nature of commitment.

THE NATURE OF COMMITMENT

Our first observation about commitment is the fact that it is unavoidable. In a previous chapter we had occasion to note that every human being, by virtue of his physical and social environment, is repeatedly required to commit himself to some particular course of action.[32] Harry Lauder has vividly personalized this universal experience in one of his popular songs:

> "Oh, it's nice to get up in the morning,
> But it's nicer to lie in bed."[33]

At the moment of awakening consciousness I may proceed to arise immediately. Or I may choose to delay the act of rising. Meanwhile a variety of motives comes into play and ultimately one more dominant than the others accelerates or inhibits action. In any case

I have committed myself. This commitment involves both physical and social consequences. Repeated acts of commitment of a certain type may lead to the formation of habits, in which case moral consequences also are involved. The wisdom of Proverbs recognizes such consequences:

> "Yet a little sleep, a little slumber,
> A little folding of the hands to sleep:
> So shall thy poverty come as a robber,
> And thy want as an armed man."[34]

My act of commitment may not be conscious or deliberate. I may be quite unaware of the forces which operate in this commitment. I may deliberately allow events to mold me as they will. But even this attitude involves commitment; that is, I am committed not to commit myself! "At every level of human experience," as Theodore Meyer Greene has shown, "adaptation to environment, participation in the temporal process, and positive commitment are unavoidable."[35]

A second observation about commitment is its complexity. The life of every man is an arena in which ideas, motives, and causes battle to gain controlling ascendancy over the whole man. How well Victor Hugo has described that conflict: "There, beneath the external silence [of the human face], are combats of giants, as in Homer; melees of dragons and hydras, and clouds of phantoms as in Milton; ghostly labyrinths as in Dante. What a gloom enwraps that infinite which each man bears within himself, and by which he measures in despair the desires of his will and the actions of his life!"[36]

We are now prepared to make still a third observation about commitment: its relation to freedom. In considering how Scripture contributes to the awakening, freeing, and expanding of human consciousness, no aspect is more vital than this connection between commitment and freedom to think. How is it that Holy Scripture is so ideally suited to act as an instrument of introducing light into the abyss of human illusion and of freeing the mind to exercise its normal function in personality?

No one has described this function of Scripture more correctly than Richard C. Trench: "Scripture is in no way a record of man's various attempts to cure himself of the deep wound of his soul; it is no history of the experiments which man makes, as he looks around him to see if he may find on earth medicinal herbs that will meet his need; but it presents man already in an hospital of souls, and under a divine treatment . . . Holy Scripture . . . is the history of men in a constitution; a history of men not seeking relations with God, but men having such relations, and whose task is now to believe in these relations, and to maintain them."[37] The adequacy of Scripture to release men from intellectual bondages consists in the fact that it is much more than a history of revelation. Scripture is a presentation of the histories of souls, souls who have responded or who have failed to respond adequately to revelation. This is seen most clearly in the relations between Jesus and His disciples. What constitutes the most distinctive note of the New Testament, according to E. P. Dickie, is the fact that there we find in Jesus Christ "the pattern of true faith in God the Father . . . In Him revelation and response go hand in hand. In Jesus we see the perfect response, and, because of that, also the perfect revelation."[38] This brings us to the vital center of our subject.

JESUS' CALL TO COMMITMENT AND ITS RELATION TO FREEDOM

The pattern of the Synoptic Gospels is shaped about the attempt of Jesus to win from His disciples a decisive response to the revelation of His own person which was being made by His words and deeds. From the moment when "the Pharisees went out, and straightway with the Herodians took counsel against him, how they might destroy him,"[39] it became Jesus' concern to win, to form, and to train a small group of disciples who were committed to His cause.

He gathered about Him twelve chosen disciples. By personal association as well as by public discourse, by parable, and by mighty
work, He appealed to their susceptibilities until at length they came
to Cæsarea Philippi.[40] Here he seized the opportunity afforded by a
moment of retirement to disclose a new element in His teaching: the
all-embracing principle of basal self-commitment.

He began by asking them a general question: "Who do men say
that I am?" When they replied, "John the Baptist; and others,
Elijah; but others, One of the prophets," He probed more deeply
and asked, "But who say ye that I am?" Peter answered and said,
"Thou art the Christ." Without any delay Jesus proceeded to unfold the meaning of this confession.

First, He charged them to tell no man. It would not do *now* to
proclaim His Messiahship publicly and thus to intensify the malignity of the Jewish leaders, or to invoke the wrath of the Romans. The
time had not yet come to proclaim the whole truth of the Messianic
secret publicly.

Second, He began to teach them what kind of Messiah He was
to be. Ignoring the title Peter had used, "Thou art the Christ,"
Jesus took up instead a title He alone always uses in the Gospels in
reference to Himself, Son of man. "The Son of man," said He,
"must suffer many things, and be rejected by the elders, and the
chief priests, and the scribes, and be killed, and after three days rise
again." Suffer, be rejected, be killed, rise again. What strange
words for their Messiah to use! How heavily these words must have
fallen upon the ears of these disciples. Peter, at least, objected stren-
uously. He rebuked Jesus. His Messiah was to reign, not to suffer;
He was to be acclaimed, not to be rejected; He was to come in
glory, not to be killed. As for rising again, what could He mean by
that? Peter could not think of the Messiah in the role Jesus had just
described. Peter's natural craving for personal power, his characteristic preference for the safe side, his human bias in favor of himself,
all rebelled against such ignominy for Jesus. Certainly all this should
never come to Him! But Jesus vehemently set aside this rebuke,

saying to Peter, "Thou mindest not the things of God, but the things of men." Our English word "mindest" is entirely too tame an equivalent for the word of Jesus. It means literally "to take sides." Peter, "You do not side with God, but with men."[41] Peter, you do not look at things as God does, but as men regard them. You must think about Me on a different level from that dictated by human self-interest. I am committed to a course of action which involves utter giving of Myself.

Third, having declared His own personal intention Jesus now summoned to self-commitment those who would be His disciples. In the presence of the multitudes He declared: "If any man would come after me, let him deny himself, and take up his cross, and follow me." Jesus based this call upon a paradox. To save one's life is to lose it; to lose one's life is to save it. To gain the whole world and yet forfeit one's life is profitless, for what can a man give in exchange for his life? In other words, Jesus was seeking to set these men free from the paralysis of self-rule by making them willing to accept instead the rule of God. In due time Jesus would in very deed come in the glory of His Father. The kingdom of God veritably would come with power. However, the acceptance of God's rule for their lives meant thinking not merely about Him but from Him, as from a new center. It meant abandoning the quest of the self-sustained life and finding instead enlargement of life in the kingdom of God. Living in the kingdom of God meant making God the center of all their relations. Jesus was attempting to make these men see that making up their minds about Him actually involved first making up their minds about themselves. Where truly did their personal loyalties lie? Jesus knew that personal commitment and personal freedom go hand in hand. Jesus knew that God can never be satisfied with a partial loyalty. His claims are made upon the whole man—heart, soul, mind, and strength.

How then can the individual really be free, free to live, free to think? The answer is made obvious by practical experience. The degree of real freedom enjoyed by an individual depends upon that to which he is committed. He is free to choose whom he will serve.

We may therefore conclude this study by considering two phases of experience in which commitment is involved. First, freedom to think without commitment, and second, commitment without freedom to think.

FREEDOM TO THINK WITHOUT COMMITMENT

In individual experience the desire not to be committed is often fully as strong as the passion to be free. When an individual attempts to maintain his personal freedom without committing himself to that course of action which really frees him, the tensions of bewilderment and illusion are bound to follow.

Francis Thompson has recorded his own effort to evade the great commitment:

> "I fled Him, down the nights and down the days;
>   I fled Him, down the arches of the years;
>   I fled Him, down the labyrinthine ways
>   Of my own mind; and in the mist of tears
>   I hid from Him, and under running laughter.
> . . . .
> (For, though I knew His love Who followèd,
>   Yet was I sore adread
>   Lest, having Him, I must have naught beside.)"[42]

It has been said that the very fog has its fascination for the man who has no serious wish to go home! One of the primary functions of Holy Scripture is to turn human desires homeward. By what a wealth of exalted imagery does Holy Scripture seek to lay hold of the mind that loves to wander, picturing the city that hath foundations, whose builder and maker is God; the security of the one who dwells in the secret place of the Most High, and abides under the shadow of the Almighty; the comfort in the house of many mansions; the Father's unrestrained love for the prodigal; the good Shepherd's untiring search for the sheep; the peace of God which passeth all understanding; the glorious throne set on high from the beginning, which is the place of our sanctuary! But all this wealth of imagery and its meaning is lost unless the mind to which it is presented takes it seriously. In one of his most self-revealing confessions Leslie Stephen says: "My own experience is, I imagine, a common one. When I ceased to accept the teachings of my youth, it was not so much a process of giving up beliefs, as of discovering that I had never really believed. The contrast between the genuine convictions that guide and govern conduct, and the professions which we were taught to repeat in church, when once realized, was too glaring. One belonged to the world of realities, and the other to the world of dreams."[43]

"I was not discovering that my creed was false, but that I had never really believed it. I had unconsciously imbibed the current phraseology; but the formulæ belonged to the superficial stratum of my thought instead of to the fundamental convictions. I will not inquire what is the inference as to my intellectual development. I fear that it would be rather humiliating, or at least imply that the working of 'what I pleased to call my mind' had been of a very easygoing and perfunctory character."[44] Here is the typical case of a modern man abandoning the teachings of his youth not because they were not substantially true but because they inhibited his freedom to think. As a youth he had learned words without embracing the genuine convictions they represent. According to his own testimony these words were never written upon his heart. Such easygoing, perfunctory acquiescence to the claims of God, without being endorsed and vitalized by personal intention, could never set him free from himself. The prophets understood this frame of mind. One of them says:

> "Thus saith the Lord, thy Redeemer,
> The Holy One of Israel:
> I am the Lord thy God,
> Who teacheth thee for thy profit,
> Who leadeth by the way that thou shouldest go.
> Oh that thou wouldest hearken to My commandments!
> Then would thy peace be as a river,
> And thy righteousness as the waves of the sea."[45]

No man, then, is free to think who is in bondage to himself. The Christian Gospel appeals to man's passion to be free by offering man, in Christ, the opportunity of self-commitment not merely to a cause, but to a Person. For the human heart

> ". . . has no spring of action sure—
> It varies with the wind,
> It cannot freely move
> Till Christ has wrought its chain."

Let Him enslave it with His matchless love,

> "And deathless it shall reign."[46]

It remains for us to examine one other aspect of the relation between commitment and freedom to think. What shall be said of that type of commitment which does not bear fruit in freedom?

COMMITMENT WITHOUT FREEDOM TO THINK

We live in a universe of infinitely expanding horizons. No limits can be set to the scope of man's thinking, but he must have an adequate center, a home in God. Any type of commitment, however sincere, which falls short of this personal relation eventuates in bondage, not freedom.

The most lucid example of this type of commitment in Scripture is found in the Pharisees. A. B. Davidson, in his characteristic way, once declared that Pharisaism and Deuteronomy came into the world on the same day.[47] It might have been more correct had he said that Deuteronomy and the Pharisaic interpretation of Deuteronomy came into the world together, for in Jeremiah and in Jesus, Deuteronomy found true interpreters. Professor Davidson was not referring, of course, to the Pharisaic party of Jesus' day but to the Pharisaic tendency of some of the interpreters of the great law book, who were more scrupulous over the letter than the spirit. Jeremiah observed the tendency among the people of his day to take pride in the law book as though the possession of it put them into right relations with God. "How do ye say, We are wise," he asked, "and the law of the Lord is with us."[48]

By the time the first century had arrived, Pharisaic legalism had come to full bloom. The Pharisaic party in Judaism was especially exact about the interpretation and observance of the law. So seriously did these leaders take the law, so fully were they committed to it, that they spared themselves no pain or sacrifice to fulfill it punctually according to the letter. Jesus, who came into open conflict with the Pharisees, declared, "Ye search the scriptures, because ye think that in them ye have eternal life; and these are they which bear witness of me; and ye will not come to me, that ye may have life."[49] Their very zeal for Scripture had led them into a bondage from which Jesus sought to release them.

One illustration of this bondage was their Sabbath practice. The original commandment as given in the Decalogue read, "Six days shalt thou labor, and do all thy work; but the seventh day is a sabbath unto the Lord thy God: in it thou shalt not do any work."[50] As stated, the commandment defines the keeping of this day in terms both of end and means: the end—"unto God"; the means—"not any work." The Pharisaic scribes, attracted by scrupulous adherence to the letter, went to great pains to interpret what was meant by "work," but they overlooked what is "unto God." By the first century they had succeeded in enacting 39 general prohibitions which defined what kind of activity was work. These general enactments, or chief laws (known as *abhoth*), were divided and subdivided into still further definitions which were designed to determine the range and meaning of the chief enactments. These were called the *toldoth*.[51]

The twenty-first and twenty-second general enactments in the Sabbath law prohibited the tying or the untying of a knot. These provisions were too indefinite, however, for Pharisaic zeal. They required corollaries to make them specific and these the doctors of the law supplied. According to Tract *Shabbath*, "the following are the knots, the making of which renders a man guilty: The knot of camel-drivers and that of sailors; and as one is guilty by reason of tying, so also of untying them . . . Guilt is not incurred by reason of a knot, which can be untied with one hand. There are knots by reason of which one is not guilty as one is in the case of the camel-driver's and sailor's knots. A woman may tie up a slit in her shift and the strings of her cap, those of her girdle, the straps of the shoes and sandals, of skins of wine and oil, of a pot with meat . . . And to tie strings of the girdle being permitted, it was agreed that a pail also might be tied over the well with a girdle, but not with a rope."[52]

The human mind is capable of the most subtle casuistries. The Pharisees had fallen prey to this peril, confusing means with end. They were fully committed to finding an answer to the question, What is work? They ignored the crucial question, What is unto God? It was this question which Jesus insisted they should face. Reorientation of life, in terms of God and His ways, would not only throw new light on the meaning of work, but would deliver them from a yoke of bondage more grievous to be borne than any which the Romans had devised.

Commitment to any course of action which falls short of glorifying God and of enjoying Him forever leads inevitably to bondage, not freedom. Holy Scripture—the Word of God—is a means of instruction, not an idol to be worshiped. We may well pray to be delivered from the twofold peril to which men who aspire to be free are always subject: From the passion to be free to think, without commitment; and from commitment to aught but Thee, good Lord, deliver us!

NOTES

The first quotation on the title page of this chapter is from John Alfred Faulkner, "English Bible Translations," in *The Biblical Review,* April, 1924, p. 202. The second quotation is attributed to Descartes.

1. Victor Hugo, *Les Miserables, Fantine,* Book vii, 3.
2. Isaiah 1:2, 3.
3. Isaiah 1:4, 5.
4. *Cf.* Proverbs 23:7.
5. Philippians 4:8, 9.
6. Parmenides III, 249.
7. See, for instance, Locke, *Essay Concerning Human Understanding,* II, viii, 9. "Whatsoever the mind perceives in itself, or is the immediate object of perception, thought, or understanding, that I call *idea." Cf.* Berkeley, *Human Knowledge,* I, 29; and Hume, *Treatise of Human Nature,* I, i, 1.
8. See article entitled *Oldsters and Youngsters,* by George E. Sokolsky, New York *Herald Tribune,* March 1, 1937, p. 12.
9. Woodrow Wilson, *The New Freedom,* pp. 282, 283. Doubleday, Page and Co., New York, 1913.
10. Genesis, chapters 2 and 3.
11. Genesis 39:9.
12. Exodus 16:1-3.
13. I Kings, chapter 18.
14. Jeremiah 2:13.
15. Mark 2:1—3:6; Luke 5:17—6:11.
16. Galatians, chapter 2.
17. Revelation 3:20.
18. Mark 12:29-31.
19. *E.g.* Deuteronomy 5:2; 6:1-3.
20. Driver, *Deuteronomy.* International Critical Commentary, p. 91. Scribners, 1895.
21. Deuteronomy 6:3.
22. Deuteronomy 6:10-12.
23. See, for instance, Driver, *op. cit.,* p. 91.
24. The answer to the first question of the Shorter Catechism.
25. Matthew 4:1-11; Luke 4:1-13.
26. Proverbs 9:10; *cf.* 1:7; 15:33.
27. Matthew 4:7; Luke 4:12.
28. Deuteronomy 6:16.
29. Exodus 17:1-7.
30. Deuteronomy 6:17-19. A splendid example of such filial piety is found in Robert Burns, "A Cotter's Saturday Night."
31. Mark 12:29-31.
32. Chapter Two, pp. 52-55.
33. Last lines of a song by Harry Lauder called "It's Nice to Get Up in the Morning." (1913.)
34. Proverbs 6:10, 11; *cf.* 24:33, 34.
35. Theodore Meyer Greene, *The Arts and the Art of Criticism,* p. 237.

THESE WORDS UPON THY HEART

36. Victor Hugo, *Les Miserables*, Fantine, Book vi, 3.
37. Richard C. Trench, *Hulsean Lectures*, pp. 28, 29.
38. E. P. Dickie, *Revelation and Response*, p. 253.
39. Mark 3:6; Luke 6:11.
40. Mark 8:27—9:1; Matthew 16:13-28; Luke 9:18-27.
41. Goodspeed Translation.
42. *The Complete Poetical Works of Francis Thompson*, The Modern Library, p. 88.
43. *Social Rights and Duties*, The Ethical Library, Vol. 1, p. 12. I am indebted for this reference to Olin A. Curtis, *Personal Submission to Jesus Christ*.
44. "Some Early Impressions" in *National Review*, October, 1903, p. 214. This reference and the preceding may also be found in *The Life and Letters of Leslie Stephen*, by Frederik William Maitland, pp. 133, 134. G. B. Putnam's Sons, New York, 1906.
45. Isaiah 48:17, 18. *A New Translation of the Old Testament*, The Jewish Publication Society of America, Philadelphia.
46. George Matheson, hymn entitled, "Make Me a Captive, Lord." (Altered.)
47. A. B. Davidson, Article, Jeremiah, in Hastings' *Dictionary of the Bible*, Vol. II, p. 577.
48. Jeremiah 8:8, 9.
49. John 5:39, 40.
50. Exodus 20:8-11.
51. See Emil Schürer, *A History of the Jewish People in the Time of Jesus Christ*, Second Division, Vol. II, pp. 96*ff*. Charles Scribner's Sons, New York.
52. Tract *Shabbath*, xv, 1, 2. For a good recent translation into English, see *The Babylonian Talmud*, Edited by I. Epstein. The Soncino Press, London, 1935.

TRANSLATING SCRIPTURE INTO ACTION

> *"To restore a commonplace truth to its first uncommon lustre, you need only translate it into action. But to do this you must first have reflected on its truth."*
> —*S. T. Coleridge.*

Translating Scripture Into Action

ౘ

THE NEED OF A CHART

ALONG THE JAMES RIVER between Richmond and Newport News, the United States Coast Guard maintains a system of tall beacon lights. As the pilot of a boat comes around a bend of the river, he spies the beacon directly ahead. By a turn of the wheel he adjusts the course of his ship in the direction of that beacon until the next signal comes into view. By following the successive signals his ship is kept in the center of the channel and so avoids the shallows to the left or to the right on either side. Every river pilot learns from experience how far he can deviate from dead reckoning and still enjoy the freedom of the river. His success as a navigator rests upon a twofold principle of action. First, he must keep the beacon lights always in view; second, he must adjust his course to the position of the beacon. This same principle of action is utilized by the air pilot, who adjusts the instruments of his plane to the course charted by the radio beam and so flies straight through the darkness to his destination or makes a safe landing although shrouded by fog.

At first thought it might appear to be oversimplifying human experience to suggest that there is any possible analogy between a river pilot and the individual who must chart his course in the stream of life. One sympathizes with Thomas H. Huxley in his search for a satisfying principle of action. In his address on Descartes, "Discourse Touching the Method of Using One's Reason Lightly and of Seeking Scientific Truth," he declared, "I protest that if some great Power would agree to make me always think what is true and do what is right, on condition of being turned into a sort of clock and wound up every morning before I got out of bed, I should instantly close with the offer. The only freedom I care about is the freedom to do right; the freedom to do wrong I am ready to part with on the cheapest terms to anyone who will take it of me."[1]

If Huxley's suggestion were possible, it would indeed oversimplify the problem of human existence. But man is not a clock to be wound up every morning before he gets out of bed, nor is it possible for him to enjoy the freedom to do right apart from the freedom also to do wrong. His very constitution as a free moral agent requires that he shall act as he chooses and that he shall bear the consequences of his acts. What complicates the drama of every individual's personal experience, however, is the fact that he does not live unto himself alone. He implicates others in his actions and others entangle him in theirs. Every individual's own interior life is far too complicated and his human relations are far too intricate for him ever to measure his acts with precision on any calculated basis of right or wrong. If he preferred, a river pilot could make soundings to keep his ship in the channel, but for the individual person in modern society the stream of life moves far too swiftly, its current is often against him, and its eddies and rapids and hidden shoals are far too treacherous for safe navigation without a surer and more authoritative chart of action than external soundings.

THE LIGHT OF SCRIPTURE AND THE RULE OF GOD

With what poignant words the Apostle Paul described this antimony of human experience when he declared, "I cannot be good as I desire to be, and I do wrong against my wishes."[2] And with what deft but pathetic strokes the prophet Jeremiah pictured the tragedy of his own people in his memorable words, "Yea, the stork in the heavens knoweth her appointed times; and the turtle-dove and the swallow and the crane observe the time of their coming; but my people know not the law of the Lord."[3] Jeremiah's word for *law* here is *mishpāṭ,* for which a number of English equivalents have been suggested: custom, rule, ordinance, ethic, order, manner of life.[4] What Jeremiah deplored was the disloyalty of his people to this *mishpāṭ,* this rule of God; their failure to respond to the manner of life which corresponds to His nature. The birds attend no schools but are not without instruction; they have no maps but know their route; they consult no almanacs yet keep their dates. They observe as by instinct the unwritten law of nature, but man made in the image of his Creator disregards "God's fresh heavenward will" with his "poor earthward striving";[5] or, he ignores the higher guidance of conscience and revealed truth. Scripture like a light that shines in a dark place corresponds to the river beacon or the radio beam, the only rule—as the Westminster Divines put it— "to direct us how we may glorify and enjoy" God. In the familiar lines of Bishop How, Holy Scripture

> ". . . shineth like a beacon
> Above the darkling world.
> It is the chart and compass
> That o'er life's surging sea,
> 'Mid mists and rocks and quicksands,
> Still guides, O Christ, to Thee."

The primary problem, then, of every man is to find true clues which indicate the manner of his adjustment to God. What is the deepest and most assertive thing in him? What obtrudes itself most persistently and powerfully in his living? What is the bent of his will? To what ultimate end is his life committed? When a man, under the urgency of circumstance, becomes a real problem to himself and is desperately in earnest about finding his way, and turns to Scripture, light veritably does arise in the darkness. In the Old Testament Scriptures he finds a true mirror of life embodying centuries of available spiritual wisdom. Particularly is this true of the Psalms, which Calvin characteristically called "the Anatomy of all the parts of the soul, for not an affection will anyone find in himself, an image of which is not reflected in this mirror."[6] He finds a collection of concrete life situations which exhibit a variety of experiences in which causes and effects are traced with profound illumination. Here the characters of good men and evil men are portrayed with vividness for his instruction and interpreted in the light of God and His ways.

But Scripture which mirrors life also requires life as the only adequate response. In the Gospels of the New Testament the reader finds the words and deeds of Christ's perfect life presented in terms of response to the Father's will. He observes how "the great ideas that were regulative of the Old Testament revelation were also those which guided the practice and conduct of our Lord."[7] He is led to reflect how "all the light of sacred story" gathers round His head sublime, who died on the cross for his sins and was raised from the dead for his justification. In the Epistles he finds the life and teachings of Christ interpreted and applied to concrete situations in personal life, home life, Christian brotherhood, civic and public affairs. In the Revelation, in spite of its enigmatic pictures, he finds the commonplace illuminated by the spirit of worship. This transcript of life in Holy Scripture, which declares the *mishpāṭ* (rule) of God and proclaims the manner of response required, is indeed a chart and compass to man's chief end, the glorifying and enjoying of God. The Psalmist understood full well where a man finds true clues to himself and his destiny: "Blessed is the man that feareth the Lord, that delighteth greatly in his commandments . . . Unto the upright there ariseth light in the darkness."[8]

Attractive as the suggestion in Huxley's protest might appear to be to some people, man cannot be wound up like a clock every morning before he gets out of bed. But Scripture does invite him to close with an offer which provides a true clue to himself. This clue involves accommodating his course of action to the light of God and His *mishpāṭ*. Let us observe more closely how this offer is mediated.

THE TRANSLATION OF SCRIPTURE

The Bible is the most translated book in the world. According to the most recent statistics made available by the American Bible Society, the number of languages into which some part or all of the Bible has been translated is a total of 1068. By means of translation Holy Scripture crosses all barriers of language to people of every race. This remarkable adaptability of the Scriptures to the multitude of human dialects and languages is an eloquent witness to the elemental nature of its speech. Steeped in Oriental customs and expressed in Oriental modes of thought, it is much more than an Oriental book. As a true mirror of life it speaks a universal language. The book itself is immeasurably greater than any of its modes of expression, for as a vehicle of communication it is deep calling unto deep.

Woodrow Wilson once said: "When you have read the Bible you will know that it is the word of God, because you will have found it the key to your own heart, your own happiness, and your own duty."[9] In a more simple and direct way a native African is said to have declared, "The Bible tells me my heart." Into whatever tongue it may be translated Holy Scripture speaks the language of the human heart. It is one thing, however, to find in Scripture the key to one's own happiness and duty; it is another to turn the key to effective advantage, for the human heart may resist as well as respond to its truth. What kind of translation, then, is required to cross this barrier?

By derivation, our English word translate (from the Latin, *translatus,* pp. *transferre*—"to bring over, carry over, transfer") means literally, "to turn from one language into another." The effective speech of the human heart is action rather than words. Thoreau. who understood this, once declared, "At first blush, a man is not capable of reporting truth. To do that he must be drenched and saturated with it. Then the truth will exhale from him naturally."[10] The ultimate translation of Scripture, then, is not a book or a page but a life. "Ye are epistles," wrote the Apostle Paul to the Corinthians. "Ye are our epistle, written in our hearts, known and read of all men."[11] When his authority as an apostle was called into question, Paul was ready to allow the truth for which he lived to be vindicated by the manner in which it was expressed by the Corinthian Christians, as living epistles. A slightly different way of stating the same idea, but one equally remarkable for its suggestiveness, is the Johannine phrase "doing truth." "If we say that we have fellowship with him and walk in darkness, we lie, and do not the truth."[12] The same idea is put in a more positive way, "But he that doeth the truth cometh to the light."[13] To *do truth* is to live it out. Right action, in John's view, is true thought realized in active personal experience. The one universal language known and understood by all men is action. An accomplished fact is the most potent word.

SCRIPTURE AND THE SPRINGS OF ACTION

Right action is true thought made operative in a living person. How is this potency of truth transmuted into personal activity? Coleridge answered that this is accomplished through the instrumentality of words. For, according to Coleridge, "words are not things, they are living powers by which the things of most importance to mankind are actuated, combined, and humanized."[14] What, then, shall be said of the manner in which words of Scripture are taken upon the heart? Coleridge answers, "To restore a commonplace truth to its first uncommon lustre, you need only translate it into action. But to do this you must first have reflected on its truth." Coleridge is even more specific. He adds, "The one sure way of giving freshness and importance to commonplace truths is to reflect on them in direct reference to our own state and conduct, to our own past and future being."[15] In other words, re-creation of truth takes place only as the individual converts the living power of words of truth into personal intention and practice. Only so does truth pass through him living and intact. Let us consider three aspects of this process: first, Scripture and an individual's moods; second, Scripture as an uplifting power in conscious choice; third, Scripture and the individual at prayer.

Scripture and an Individual's Moods

The ultimate test of Christian faith, as Robert Freeman asserted, lies not in its replies to our questions but in its answer to our cravings. And the reason for this is obvious. Since man is more than mind, his feelings as well as his thoughts must have some sure ground of confidence if the life is to be whole and stable. And the adequacy of Scripture as an effective instrument for awakening and nurturing Christian faith lies in the way it meets a man at the level of his deepest yearnings. No one will question the primordial character of feeling as an essential element in conscious life, or its profound influence over thought and action. Schleiermacher placed such extraordinary emphasis upon this aspect of consciousness that he defined religion as essentially the feeling of conscious dependence.[16] A valid criticism of Schleiermacher's view is that it falls short of any adequate definition of religion. Yet it would hardly be too much to say that no definition of religion or of faith which ignores the feelings could be said to be adequate. For the feelings unquestionably are a spring and fount of action. But they must never become an end of action. And this is why the feelings must be brought under the control of some determining voice which resides above and beyond mere individual grasp. No man is wise enough, good enough, or honest enough to interpret his own moods to himself with confidence. His feelings arise from depths of his being which are too abysmal, too self-assertive, too contradictory, to offer a valid basis of correct judgment or introspection. Conflicting motives, impulses, and reasons compete with each other until brought under the influence of a single eye other than his own.

Rudolph Otto has defined this reality as the "wholly-other." The corresponding "creature-feeling," on the part of the individual, "is the emotion of a creature, abased and overwhelmed by its own nothingness, in contrast to that which is supreme above all creatures." This object outside the self Otto identifies as "the numinous."[17] Isaac Watts has described this "numinous" as an

> "Eternal Power! whose high abode
> Becomes the grandeur of a God;
> Infinite lengths beyond the bounds
> Where stars revolve their little rounds.
>
> . . . . . .
>
> Earth from afar has heard Thy fame,
> And worms have learned to lisp Thy name:
> But oh the glories of Thy mind
> Leave all our soaring thoughts behind."[18]

Among its most characteristic notes two in particular indicate how supremely Scripture is qualified to act as an effective instrument in the process of converting the feelings into intentional and deliberate action. They are the positive confessional character of Scripture, and its disclosure of a true perspective of life in which God initiates righteous action. While these major notes are not equally obvious everywhere, they are so characteristic of Scripture as a whole in its appeal to the feelings that we may well consider each in turn. And we can do no better than to observe how the first of these is expressed in a typical passage, the 16th Psalm.

I. THE POSITIVE CONFESSIONAL NOTE

Observe the personal, conversational character of the 16th Psalm. Here is a man who has found immediate, intimate access to God:

> "In thee do I take refuge."
> "Thou art my Lord."
> "I have no good beyond thee."

This individual speaks as a priest in his own right.

> "The Lord is the portion of mine inheritance,
>   and of my cup."

Like the Levites who received no land but whose estate was God Himself, so, too, this person recognizes God as His own abiding possession. For him life's cup is full, for no experience can equal that which comes through converse with God. But observe carefully that God Himself, rather than anything God gives or does, is the clue to his satisfaction: "The Lord is the portion of mine inheritance, and of my cup . . . Yea, I have a goodly heritage." The speaker here is possessed by one supreme, undeniable reality. Like the pilgrim in the 23rd Psalm who can say, "The Lord is *my* shepherd; *I* shall not want"; or like Mary of Bethany who in contrast to her busy sister Martha, cumbered and oppressed with much serving, had found the one thing which is needful, "that good part, which shall not be taken away";[19] or like Paul who could say, "This one thing I do";[20] or like the individual described by Jesus in the Sermon on the Mount whose eye is single, and therefore whose whole body is full of light,[21] this person had found the one enkindling, animating flame of living devotion which transforms feeling into intention, "Thou art my Lord: I have no good beyond thee."

Now what gives this positive note peculiar urgency is the sense of pressing need with which the Psalm begins: "Preserve me, O God; for in thee do I take refuge." What serious person can fail to recognize here the nature of this tension? How well Mr. Miller, the wise counsellor of Thomas Chalmers, understood it when young Chalmers as a youth of seventeen came to him at St. Andrews, in a state of great excitement and unhappiness. "He was earnestly searching for the truth," says Mr. Miller, "but he could not find his way . . . Those who were not particularly acquainted with him thought him going fast into a state of derangement. One very common expression in his public prayers which showed the state of his mind at that time—'Oh, give us some steady object for our mind to rest upon'— was uttered with all his characteristic earnestness and emphasis."[22]

The first and primary function of Scripture is to disclose this "wholly other," this Eternal Power, who in a world of variableness and change is the only steady object upon which the seeking mind, the yearning heart, may rest with confidence. And this is done in such a comprehensive manner, within the broad scope of its appeal, that there is hardly a human mood to which Scripture does not speak a discerning and understanding word. The person who has committed himself to live by Scripture—that is, to adopt the role of agent and actually to participate in the stream of life which Scripture unfolds—finds inevitably, within its broad scope, ample appeals to his varying and changing moods. This stabilizing process, by which the inner life is brought into a state of adjustment with itself under illumination of Scripture and so released for right action, is characterized by a second distinctive note: the disclosure of a true perspective of life in which God initiates righteous action.

2. A TRUE PERSPECTIVE OF LIFE

There is a great deal of confusion abroad concerning the basic unity of the Bible. The fact that the Bible is divided into two general parts, the Old Testament and the New Testament, has given rise to the popular impression that there are really two kinds of religion in the Bible or, at least, two different dispensations, a dispensation of Law and a dispensation of Grace. A. B. Davidson has given wise and discriminating counsel concerning the error of this popular notion. "We must beware," says he, "of speaking of the law as a dispensation or economy of salvation. The distinction between the old and the new dispensations is not that of law and gospel, but that of promise of the gospel—in itself essentially a gospel—and the gospel. Subjectively, the two dispensations are one; they differ, mainly, in the amount and clearness of objective truth enjoyed."[23]

In order to emphasize and to clarify this essential oneness of Biblical revelation, Adolf Deissmann introduced the use of the word *cult.* In our own popular usage, the word cult is applied as a practical equivalent for a sect or for some specific form of religious experience followed by a particular group. To designate such a form of experience as practiced by an organized religious body Deissmann uses the word *cultus.* But by using the word cult in its narrowest possible sense he brings into clear relief the root idea of worship as a form of action. By cult he means, "A practical dependence upon, a practical attitude toward the deity on the part of a single individual or of a community."[24] We need to keep clearly in mind that this dependence upon deity is conceived in terms of its practical nature, that is, dependence upon God is related to concrete acts of personal or collective experience.

Deissmann distinguishes between two types of cult: Acting cult and Reacting cult. "In both cases an action takes place. But in the first type the action is a spontaneous performance of the individual or of the community, intended to produce in response to it a performance on the part of the deity, effective through its own execution, effective as *actio acta,* as *opus operatum.*" That is to say, the work wrought is assumed, on the part of the individual or community, to have the inherent efficacy of a sacrament to confer grace. In this case, as an individual worshiper, I make an offering to God by some act to influence Him favorably toward me. This is Acting cult. "In the second case, the reacting type, the action of the man is an action in response, a reaction. Here it is God Himself who is really the Leitourgos, the Theourgos in the highest sense; the individual or the community only says the amen." In this case God makes the offer to me as disclosed by some action on His part to influence me favorably toward Him. Here, God takes the initiative. This is the root of Reacting cult. In the light of this distinction "the whole history of Christian religious life can be understood," says Deissmann, "as the struggle of Reacting cult against Acting cult. And this struggle had its eternal exemplar in the conflict between Law and Faith, which Paul lived through and wrestled through."[25] Thomas Huxley was in search of a principle of action which would give him freedom to do right. He was ready to part with the freedom to do wrong on any terms. Scripture discloses a principle of action which neither makes man an automaton nor does violence to his freedom. This root distinction between Acting cult and Reacting cult is very fruitful in its manner of suggesting where the mainspring of action is really found. The central unity of the Bible consists in its presentation of God's approach to man. God is the Seeker, man the Found. God makes the offering, man accepts the offer. There are not two kinds of true religion taught in the Bible but one. At bottom the religion which the Bible approves is the religion of divine grace: the religion of Reacting cult.

It is true that ethical standards of action are presented in both the Old and New Testaments, as in the Decalogue and in the Sermon on the Mount. The ethical qualities thus represented are reckoned in Scripture as the consequent of something else, not as the ground of man's righteousness before God. Let us view more closely how Scripture acts as an instrument of uplifting power in personal life.

Scripture as a Power in Conscious Choice

The distinctive note of the Bible, its vital principle, as we have previously observed, is not its code but its motive.[26] Its central emphasis is that man comes to his true glory only in self-sacrificing and helpful love as a response, a reaction, to God's love. Any lesser expression of personal or collective life, no matter what achievement may be connected with it, makes a man, as Paul observed, but "as sounding brass, or a tinkling cymbal."[27] This is why decision and choice are always crucial in Christian experience.

How, then, does this appeal of Scripture to motive operate in the individual as an incentive to realize his full Christian manhood? When a possible course of action opens up which an individual recognizes to be right but which his inclinations offer powerful suggestions not to take, he experiences what Olin A. Curtis has called "the consciousness of pressure in motive."[28] Observe that this conscious pressure does not come alone from the sense of right or wrong but from his inclinations. In other words, the individual experiences ethical stress not because the voice of duty is not clear or strong, but simply because he has not made up his mind about himself. His question is, "To what or to whom shall I give my loyalty?" It is a popular but mistaken notion that a weak person experiences the greater temptation to give way to self-interest, or to satisfy the inclinations of his appetite; whereas the exact opposite is the truth. "The greater the person, the greater the clarity of self-consciousness, the greater the temptation, provided there is motive for wrong-doing."[29]

In the Epistle to the Hebrews a very illuminating expression is used to describe the personal experience of Jesus: "Who in the days of his flesh . . . though he was a Son, yet learned obedience by the things which he suffered."[30] Observe carefully that it does not say that He "learned to obey," that is, to test out the consequences of right or wrong; but rather that "he learned obedience by the things which he suffered." This does not mean that the disposition of obedience was ever lacking in Him. It does mean rather that "the disposition had to maintain itself, in the face of greater and greater demands upon it. And as He had to meet these demands rising with the tide of things which He suffered, He entered ever more deeply into the experience of what obedience was."[31] It was by His repeated and successful encounters with this conscious pressure in motive that, according to this Epistle, "he became unto all who obey him the author of eternal salvation." This pre-eminence, won at such personal cost to Himself, was used by the Epistle as a powerful inducement to strengthen the faltering loyalties of the first readers.

The First Epistle of Peter uses a similar and exceedingly suggestive expression, "children of obedience" (*tekna hupakoēs*), when speaking of Christians.[32] This expression, "children of obedience," is something vastly different from the expression, "obedient children," into which the King James Version wrongly translates this phrase.[33] How can persons be said to be children of an impersonal object, "children of obedience," unless the author means that they draw from it—that is, from obedience—the impulses or principles which mold their lives from within? Such individuals, as Professor Hort has well said, "become the visible representatives and exponents of this principle to others in their acts and speech."[34] Conduct which is ruled by a man's inclinations or desires is bound to be irregular and erratic and at the mercy of outward circumstances. What serious person cannot recall moments in his personal experience, when under conscious pressure of motive he has felt helpless to resist the dictates of desire or to repress them or keep them down? Then some word of Scripture, which flashed into his consciousness, became a rallying center of his whole being: a line from a Psalm, a turn of expression from a prophet, a word of Jesus, or a phrase from Paul. By surrendering himself to the lifting power of the higher love enshrined in that word, the solicitations of sense and the frictions of self were resolved into quietude. His mind at leisure from itself could be intent upon a higher course of action.

Let us observe two ways in which Scripture qualifies as a rallying center of personal life when translated into action by conscious choice.

1. SCRIPTURE AS A TUTOR TO THE CONSCIENCE

By conscience we mean the voice in a person which says, "You ought." Every individual has a certain power to distinguish between the right and the wrong. But it is not always possible for him to know specifically what is right and what is wrong. Even when he knows what is right, a man may refuse to do it until an overwhelming sense of personal obligation is brought home to him. And he is likely to miss this note of urgency entirely unless his mind and heart are first bathed in an atmosphere of conscious, grateful debtorship. One of the high functions of Scripture is its ability to create the climate in which such an attitude may be nurtured. This appeal to obligation and personal debtorship is one of the most common notes in the Bible. It is struck in the preface to the Ten Commandments, which properly begin, "And God spake all these words, saying, I am the Lord thy God, who brought thee out of the land of Egypt, out of the house of bondage. Thou shalt have no other gods before me," and so on.[35] The divine care of God for His people in redeeming them from slavery in Egypt is made the clear ground of their human duty. This distinctive note in the law is true also in the prophets. Micah's well-known appeal to his generation, "And what doth the Lord require of thee, but to do justly, and to love kindness, and to walk humbly with thy God?" is prefaced by the words, "He hath showed thee, O man, what is good."[36] And what had He shown to be good, but what He had already expressed in the preceding utterance? God speaks: "For I brought thee up out of the land of Egypt, and redeemed thee out of the house of bondage . . . that ye may know the righteous acts of the Lord."[37]

So, too, did Jesus appeal, in the Sermon on the Mount, by grounding the so-called "golden rule" of human relations in the Fatherhood of God: "If ye then, being evil, know how to give good gifts unto your children, how much more shall your Father who is in heaven give good things to them that ask him? All things therefore whatsoever ye would that men should do unto you, even so do ye also unto them: for this is the law and the prophets."[38] The Golden Rule as stated by Jesus is no individualistic, self-centered principle. Actually it sums up the social ideal which Jesus had been emphasizing in His preceding words as an obvious deduction. Among the "all things therefore" referred to by Jesus in this deduction, surely three are indicated in the previous context: charity, discernment, and generosity. In effect Jesus is saying, Whoever would be My disciple must exercise a charitable spirit, therefore judge others as you would like others to judge you.[39] You must use discernment in offering your gifts. Therefore prize your relations to others as you would like others to prize their relation to you.[40] Your heavenly Father is generous to them that ask Him. Therefore be generous to others as you would like others to be generous with you.[41] These words of Jesus, which sum up the Law and the Prophets into one grand utterance, relate right standards of action to their corresponding motive. As a tutor of conscience Scripture emphasizes that man comes to his true glory only in self-sacrificing, grateful love.

2. SCRIPTURE AS AN AWAKENER OF GOOD WILL

Another way in which Scripture qualifies as a lifting power in personal life is seen in its function as an awakener and quickener of good will. No blockades to good will in personal life are more potent than our prejudices, and who does not have them? Every man, as Francis Bacon suggested, looks out on life through the uncertain opening of his own den. Among the idols to which men give their allegiance, the idols of the tribe, the idols of the market place, and the idols of the theatre, Bacon included the idols of the den, by which he meant men's individual prejudices.[42] Prejudices exert a powerful influence over action. They can never be successfully corrected by reason, since usually one's prejudices are embedded deeply in the sentiments. Even Jesus did not succeed in winning over the Pharisees from their prejudices, but He showed the right way. Addressing Himself to Simon the Pharisee, who objected to the washing of His feet by the sinful woman, He told him a parable: "A certain lender had two debtors: the one owed five hundred shillings, and the other fifty. When they had not wherewith to pay, he forgave them both. Which of them therefore will love him most? Simon answered and said, He, I suppose, to whom he forgave the most. And he said unto him, Thou hast rightly judged."[43]

By this parable Jesus linked up the costliness of forgiveness with the meaning of a gracious act. For forgiveness is essentially the expression of good will on the part of a person who has been wronged to a person who has wronged him. It costs to forgive. No gift at the disposal of man is more precious than good will. By offering good will a man gives himself to another. By withholding good will a man reveals to himself and to his neighbor of what stuff he is made. An act of forgiveness, then, is the true measure of a man's generosity, and at the same time a bond which knits soul to soul. "The person who loves me most," it has been wisely observed, "is the one who knows the worst about me and still loves me." Paul could make no more effective appeal to the Ephesians than by his urging them to be "kind one to another, tenderhearted, forgiving each other, even as God also in Christ forgave" them.[44] This redemptive note of God's self-sacrificing love, made personal and real in Jesus Christ, is the most urgent claim which Scripture makes upon men in awakening good will. In his lines,

> "All I could never be,
> All men ignored in me,
> This I was worth to God,"[45]

Browning has distilled the essence of this appeal. The sense of worth to someone other than one's self is one of the most ennobling convictions which can ever be formed in a human heart. When this sense of worth is linked to the highest possible object of one's affections, the great and glorious Being who is our God, who can measure what will transpire within a human breast in the transformation of ingrained prejudices into good will? "To everyone who really experiences it," declared Willibald Herrmann, "forgiveness comes not as a matter of course, but as an astounding revelation of love."[46] In its revelation of God's love in Christ, Scripture sounds its clearest appeal to the motive of good will: man comes to his true glory only in self-sacrificing and grateful love.

There is still another way in which Scripture influences the springs of action. It is in its appeal to prayer.

Scripture and the Individual at Prayer

At first thought there appears to be no connection whatever between prayer and action. Private prayer would seem to be a function of the contemplative and secluded life. On the contrary, the most illustrious men of action presented in the pages of Scripture—Abraham and Moses; Samuel and David; Isaiah and Jeremiah; Peter (after Pentecost) and Paul; and the most illustrious of all, our Lord Jesus Christ—were pre-eminently men of prayer.

1. THE HIGHEST LEVEL OF ACTION

Viewed in terms of the totality of Scripture, prayer is the highest level of action: action which is effective because it takes its rise in the Being of God; action which on the human side represents re-action on the part of the individual in communion with God. Describing this essential relation between prayer and action, Tennyson is said to have remarked that to him prayer was like opening a sluice gate between our little channels and the great ocean, whereupon the sea gathers itself together and flows in at full tide.

Opening a sluice gate is a comparatively simple mechanical operation. But what a complex and delicate transaction it becomes when related to the spiritual and moral life of man! For in this case the sluice gate is human personality itself. And the act of praying involves not only the individual's relation to God but his relations to his brother, his neighbor, and also his enemy. Jesus was lucid and explicit in His teaching about this aspect of prayer. "If therefore thou art offering thy gift at the altar, and there rememberest that thy brother hath aught against thee, leave there thy gift before the altar, and go thy way, first be reconciled to thy brother, and then come and offer thy gift. . . . Love your enemies, and pray for them that persecute you; that ye may be sons of your Father who is in heaven."[47]

Jesus taught that to pray well one must live well. To use Tennyson's simile, what complicates the opening of the sluice gate is the life behind the prayer. "Pray can I not," cries the conscience-smitten king in *Hamlet*.

> "Pray can I not,
> Though inclination be as sharp as will.
> My stronger guilt defeats my strong intent,
> And, like a man to double business bound,
> I stand in pause where I shall first begin."[48]

2. PRAYER AND THE SOCIAL CONSCIENCE

After the death and resurrection of Jesus the disciples were initiated into a new experience of God and a new relation to each other, in which prayer and good works were the most characteristic features. This sense of community in their relations to each other pointed the way to the expression of this same attitude toward the world at large. Had not Jesus taught that their Heavenly Father makes His sun to rise on the evil and the good, and sends His rain on the just and unjust? This disposition to exhibit the character of God in all of their relations was without doubt what made the social conscience of the early Christians, and their praying, like two breaths exhaled from the same bosom. In fulfilling such conditions they were fused into a fellowship such as men had never before witnessed. These life relations were so real that the pagan world was compelled to comment in grudging admiration, "See how these Christians love one another."[49] The final argument for or against Christianity is and always has been people. Faulty Christians are always the argument hardest to meet. The argument of the strongest sort is made by those who translate the spirit of prayer into the wide spheres of human action; those the holy temper of whose personal relations with men makes their gifts at the altar of prayer acceptable. In unfolding this intimate relation between prayer and action, once again let us repeat: Scripture emphasizes that man comes to his true glory only in self-sacrificing, prayerful love.

SCRIPTURE AND THE CHRISTIAN RESPONSE

Broadly speaking we have been dealing with the problem of communication. Our point of view has been determined by the fact that communication between self-conscious, intelligent beings can take place only by means of an appropriate medium. "It takes two to speak the truth—one to speak and one to hear."[50] Two or more minds become fused when the revealing process has been matched by a corresponding response.

Specifically we have applied this thesis to the study of the Scriptures of the Christian faith. Our primary concern has not been to consider Scripture in terms of the theological question, In what sense is Holy Scripture divine revelation? Rather we have directed attention to its human correlate in the educative process, by seeking an answer to the question, What kind of response does divine revelation require?

Our approach, governed by practical considerations, has necessarily left many important broader aspects of the subject untouched. We have emphasized the instrumental worth of Scripture in the forming of responsible Christian character. We have made it our aim to see how the laws of communication may be profitably employed in making the human response to Scripture effective in Christian thought and action.

In Coleridge's lines entitled "Frost at Midnight," he addresses himself to his child, his "dear babe, so beautiful," who sleeps cradled by his side. He pictures "with tender gladness" what revelations the world of nature holds in store for the child: "its sky and stars," its "lakes and sandy shores," its "ancient mountain crags," and "clouds which image in their bulk both lakes and shores and mountain crags." And he continues:

> " . . . so shalt thou see and hear
> The lovely shapes and sounds intelligible
> Of that eternal language, which thy God
> Utters, who from eternity doth teach
> Himself in all, and all things in Himself.
> Great Universal Teacher! He shall mold
> Thy spirit, and by giving make it ask."

The same eyes and ears which interpret the language of the Eternal in nature are susceptible to the higher revelation of God's Fatherhood in the Eternal Word. So may we pray that the great

Giver will mold our spirits, as our eyes are opened and we receive His words upon our hearts.

NOTES

The quotation on the title page is from S. T. Coleridge, *Aids to Reflection,* Aphorism 2.

1. Thomas H. Huxley, *Lay Sermons, Addresses, and Reviews,* p. 373. Macmillan and Co., London, 1870.
2. Romans 7:19, Moffatt's Translation. From *THE BIBLE, A New Translation,* by James Moffatt. Harper and Brothers, publishers.
3. Jeremiah 8:7.
4. See John Skinner, *Prophecy and Religion,* p. 139, note 1. Cambridge University Press, 1922.
5. From James Russell Lowell, "Longing."
6. Calvin, *Commentary on the Psalms,* Preface, Vol. I, p. vi.
7. As for instance in Matthew 3:15. See A. W. Vernon, *The Religious Value of the Old Testament in the Light of Modern Scholarship,* pp. 80, 81. T. Y. Crowell and Co., New York, 1907.
8. Psalm 112:1-4.
9. As reported in *The Holy Bible,* Grosset and Dunlap, New York. Notes, p. 1058.
10. *The Journal of Henry David Thoreau,* Edited by H. G. O. Blake, Vol. VII, p. 189. Houghton, Mifflin and Co., Riverside Press, 1892.
11. II Corinthians 3:2.
12. I John 1:6.
13. John 3:21.
14. S. T. Coleridge, *op. cit.,* p. 65.
15. *Ibid.* Introductory Aphorisms, 2 and 3.
16. Schleiermacher's chief theological work is *Der christliche Glaube nach den Grundsätzen der evangelischen Kirche* (Second Edition 1830-31), where these views are expounded. English readers are referred to the translation of the second German edition, *The Christian Faith,* edited by H. R. Mackintosh and J. S. Stewart, Edinburgh: T. & T. Clark, 1928, especially pp. 5-18. An able review of recent criticism of Schleiermacher's views is *Types of Modern Theology,* by H. R. Mackintosh, pp. 31-100. Nisbet and Co., Ltd., London, 1942.
17. Rudolph Otto, *The Idea of the Holy,* Translated by John W. Harvey, pp. 10, 11. The Oxford Book Shelf, Oxford University Press, New York, 1939.
18. *The Psalms and Hymns of Rev. Isaac Watts.* Rippon's Selections, p. 745. J. B. Lippincott, Philadelphia, 1843.
19. Luke 10:38-42.
20. Philippians 3:13. (King James Version.)
21. Matthew 6:22.
22. James C. Moffat, *Life of Thomas Chalmers,* Second Edition, p. 20. Newman and Ivinson, New York, 1853.
23. A. B. Davidson, *Biblical and Literary Essays,* Second Edition, pp. 11, 12. Hodder and Stoughton, London, 1903.
24. Adolf Deissmann, *Paul, A Study in Social and Religious History.* Translated by Wm. E. Wilson. Second Edition, pp. 117, 118. George H. Doran and Co., New York, 1927.

25. *Ibid.*, p. 119.
26. See Chapter One, p. 9.
27. I Corinthians 13:1.
28. Olin A. Curtis, *The Christian Faith*, p. 248.
29. *Ibid.*, p. 248.
30. Hebrews 5:7, 8.
31. See A. B. Davidson, *The Epistle to the Hebrews*, p. 111. T & T. Clark, Edinburgh.
32. I Peter 1:14.
33. See also the Revised Standard Version of the New Testament (1946).
34. F. J. A. Hort, *The First Epistle of Peter*, 1:1—2:17; p. 67. Macmillan, New York, 1898.
35. Exodus 20:1-3.
36. Micah 6:8.
37. Micah 6:4, 5.
38. Matthew 7:11, 12.
39. Matthew 7:1-5, 12.
40. Matthew 7:6, 12.
41. Matthew 7:7-11, 12.
42. Francis Bacon, *Novum Organum*, Book I. Aphorisms 38-44. See *The Works of Francis Bacon*, Vol. III, p. 349. Carey and Hart, Philadelphia, 1841.
43. Luke 7:41-43.
44. Ephesians 4:32.
45. Robert Browning, "Rabbi Ben Ezra."
46. Willibald Herrmann, *The Communion of the Christian with God*, p. 194. Williams and Norgate, London, 1895.
47. Matthew 5:23, 44, 45.
48. *Hamlet.* Act 3, Scene 3, lines 38-42.
49. Tertullian, *Apologeticus*, 39:7.
50. See Chapter Three, footnote 7.

APPENDIX

Ruskin's Essay on Composition

"*The main thing which we ought to teach our youth is to* SEE *something . . . The sum of what we do teach them is to* SAY *something.*"—*John Ruskin.*

INTRODUCTORY NOTE

THIS ESSAY ON COMPOSITION, by John Ruskin, is the latter half of Letter Three in his *Elements of Drawing*, published in 1857. The title—*Elements of Drawing*—is somewhat misleading. Ruskin never intended the volume to be used by artists as a manual. His chief aim was to teach young people the art of studying nature and of observing natural facts. To use his own words (Preface), he was seeking "to obtain to the utmost of the pupil's powers, a delicate method of work, such as may ensure his seeing truly."

He appeals first to the student's initiative. In Letter One he begins, "If you desire only to possess a graceful accomplishment, to be able to converse in a fluent manner about drawing . . . I cannot help you: but if you wish . . . to set down clearly, and usefully, records of such things as cannot be described in words; . . . if you wish to obtain quicker perceptions of the beauty of the natural world; if also you wish to understand the minds of great painters, and to be able to appreciate their work sincerely, seeing it for yourself, and loving it, not merely taking up the thoughts of other people about it; then I *can* help you, or, which is better, show you how to help yourself."

Next, Ruskin urges the student to exercise his own sensory and reflective powers. He emphasizes the importance of recovering what may be called "the innocence of the eye," or "infantine sight," the art of seeing things "exactly as they are."

Finally, he introduces the student to the laws of composition. To see things "exactly as they are" means that the mind must become accustomed to discover and to contemplate relations between things. For every object of nature, as well as every work of man, consists of parts so related as to form a single whole, or to perform a single function. In this Essay on Composition Ruskin therefore defines and illustrates nine of the most common ways in which parts may be arranged to form a given whole. These ways of arranging things he calls laws of composition, which laws he proceeds to expound. His work has been described by Frederick Harrison as "a masterpiece of lucid, simple, apt expression in a subject of practical handling most difficult to explain with clearness."

The Essay has proved its value far beyond the original intent of the author. People in many different walks of life profess that the practice of these laws of composition has not only quickened their own perceptions, but has perceptibly improved their powers of expression and interpretation. I am indebted to Mrs. Louise Meyer Wood, Professor of Religious Art and Architecture in The Biblical Seminary in New York, who first pointed out how effectively Ruskin's laws of composition could be used in obtaining a true and intimate understanding of the Bible. Successive generations of students bear witness to the genuine worth of that suggestion. The accompanying abridgment is reproduced by permission of E. P. Dutton and Company, publishers of Everyman's Library in which *The Elements of Drawing and Perspective* is No. 217. Grateful acknowledgment is also due to Mr. Philip R. Adams, Director of the Cincinnati Art Museum, for permission to reproduce Turner's watercolor *Coblentz Bridge*, of the Mary Hanna collection. Only a pencil sketch appears in Ruskin's Essay. The quotation on the title page of the appendix is from *Modern Painters*, 2nd Edition, Vol. 4, p. 409.

Ruskin's Essay on Composition

(ABRIDGED)

ॐ

THE MEANING OF COMPOSITION

COMPOSITION MEANS, literally and simply, putting several things together, so as to make *one* thing out of them; the nature and goodness of which they all have a share in producing. Thus a musician composes an air, by putting notes together in certain relations; a poet composes a poem, by putting thoughts and words in pleasant order; and a painter a picture, by putting thoughts, forms, and colours in pleasant order.

In all these cases, observe, an intended unity must be the result of composition. A pavior cannot be said to compose the heap of stones which he empties from his cart, nor the sower the handful of seed which he scatters from his hand. It is the essence of composition that everything should be in a determined place, perform an intended part, and act, in that part, advantageously for everything that is connected with it.

Composition, understood in this pure sense, is the type, in the arts of mankind, of the Providential government of the world. It is an exhibition, in the order given to notes, or colours, or forms, of the advantage of perfect fellowship, discipline, and contentment. In a well-composed air, no note, however short or low, can be spared, but the least is as necessary as the greatest: no note, however prolonged, is tedious; but the others prepare for, and are benefited by, its duration: no note, however high, is tyrannous; the others prepare for, and are benefited by, its exaltation: no note, however low, is overpowered; the others prepare for, and sympathise with, its humility: and the result is, that each and every note has a value in the position assigned to it, which, by itself, it never possessed, and of which, by separation from the others, it would instantly be deprived.

Similarly, in a good poem, each word and thought enhances the value of those which precede and follow it; and every syllable has a loveliness which depends not so much on its abstract sound as on its position. Look at the same word in a dictionary, and you will hardly recognise it.

Much more in a great picture; every line and colour is so arranged as to advantage the rest. None are inessential, however slight; and none are independent, however forcible. It is not enough that they truly represent natural objects; but they must fit into certain places, and gather into certain harmonious groups: so that, for instance, the red chimney of a cottage is not merely set in its place as a chimney, but that it may affect, in a certain way pleasurable to the eye, the pieces of green or blue in other parts of the picture; and we ought to see that the work is masterly, merely by the positions and quantities of these patches of green, red, and blue, even at a distance which renders it perfectly impossible to determine what the colours represent: or to see whether the red is a chimney, or an old woman's cloak; and whether the blue is smoke, sky, or water.

It seems to be appointed, in order to remind us, in all we do, of the great laws of Divine government and human polity, that composition in the arts should strongly affect every order of mind, however unlearned or thoughtless. Hence the popular delight in rhythm and metre, and in simple musical melodies. But it is also appointed that *power* of composition in the fine arts should be an exclusive attribute of great intellect. All men can more or less copy what they see, and, more or less, remember it: powers of reflection and investigation are also common to us all, so that the decision of inferiority in these rests only on questions of *degree*. A. has a better memory than B., and C. reflects more profoundly than D. But the gift of composition is not given *at all* to more than one man in a thousand; in its highest range, it does not occur above three or four times in a century.

It follows, from these general truths, that it is impossible to give rules which will enable you to compose. You might much more easily receive rules to enable you to be witty. If it were possible to be witty by rule, wit would cease to be either admirable or amusing: if it were possible to compose melody by rule, Mozart and Cimarosa need not have been born: if it were possible to compose pictures by rule, Titian and Veronese would be ordinary men. The essence of composition lies precisely in the fact of its being unteachable, in its being the operation of an individual mind of range and power exalted above others.

But though no one can *invent* by rule, there are some simple laws of arrangement which it is well for you to know, because, though they will not enable you to produce a good picture, they will often assist you to set forth what goodness may be in your work in a more telling way than you could have done otherwise; and by tracing them in the work of good composers, you may better understand the grasp of their imagination, and the power it possesses over their materials. I shall briefly state the chief of these laws.

1. The Law of Principality

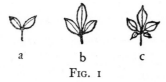

a   b   c

FIG. I

The great object of composition being always to secure unity; that is, to make out of many things one whole; the first mode in which this can be effected is, by determining that *one* feature shall be more important than all the rest, and that the others shall group with it in subordinate positions.

This is the simplest law of ordinary ornamentation. Thus the group of two leaves, *a*, Fig. I, is unsatisfactory, because it has no leading leaf; but that at *b* is prettier, because it has a head or master

• 163 •

leaf; and *c* more satisfactory still, because the subordination of the other members to this head leaf is made more manifest by their gradual loss of size as they fall back from it. Hence part of the pleasure we have in the Greek honeysuckle ornament, and such others.

Thus, also, good pictures have always one light larger or brighter than the other lights, or one figure more prominent than the other figures, or one mass of colour dominant over all the other masses. But the observance of the rule is often so cunningly concealed by the great composers, that its force is hardly at first traceable; and you will generally find they are vulgar pictures in which the law is *strikingly* manifest. This may be simply illustrated by musical melody; for instance, in such phrases as this:

One note (here the upper G) rules the whole passage, and has the full energy of it concentrated in itself. Such passages, corresponding to completely subordinated compositions in painting, are apt to be wearisome if often repeated. But in such a phrase as this:

it is very difficult to say which is the principal note. The A in the last bar is slightly dominant, but there is a very equal current of power running through the whole; and such passages rarely weary. And this principle holds through vast scales of arrangement; so that in the grandest compositions, such as Paul Veronese's Marriage in Cana, or Raphael's Disputa, it is not easy to fix at once on the principal figure; and very commonly the figure which is really chief does not catch the eye at first, but is gradually felt to be more and more conspicuous as we gaze. Thus in Titian's grand composition of the Cornaro Family, the figure meant to be principal is a youth of fifteen or sixteen, whose portrait it was evidently the painter's object to make as interesting as possible. But a grand Madonna, and a St. George with a drifting banner, and many figures more, occupy the centre of the picture, and first catch the eye; little by little we are led away from them to a gleam of pearly light in the lower corner, and find that, from the head which it shines upon, we can turn our eyes no more.

As, in every good picture, nearly all laws of design are more or less exemplified, it will, on the whole, be an easier way of explaining them to analyse one composition thoroughly, than to give instances from various works. I shall therefore take one of Turner's simplest; which will allow us, so to speak, easily to decompose it, and illustrate each law by it as we proceed.

In Fig. 2 we see the old bridge over the Moselle at Coblentz, the town of Coblentz on the right, Ehrenbreitstein on the left. The leading or master feature is, of course, the tower on the bridge. It is kept from being *too* principal by an important group on each side of it; the boats, on the right, and Ehrenbreitstein beyond. The boats are large in mass, and more forcible in colour, but they are broken into small divisions, while the tower is simple, and therefore it still leads. Ehrenbreitstein is noble in its mass, but so reduced by aerial perspective of colour that it cannot contend with the tower, which therefore holds the eye, and becomes the key of the picture. We shall see presently how the very objects which seem at first to contend with it for the mastery are made, occultly, to increase its pre-eminence.

2. *The Law of Repetition*

Another important means of expressing unity is to mark some kind of sympathy among the different objects, and perhaps the pleasantest, because most surprising, kind of sympathy, is when one group imitates or repeats another; not in the way of balance or symmetry, but subordinately, like a far-away and broken echo of it. Prout has insisted much on this law in all his writings on composition; and I think it is even more authoritatively present in the minds of most great composers than the law of principality. In the composition I have chosen for our illustration, this reduplication is employed to a singular extent. The tower, or leading feature, is first repeated by the low echo of it to the left; put your finger over this lower tower, and see how the picture is spoiled. Then the spires of Coblentz are all arranged in couples (how they are arranged in reality does not matter; when we are composing a great picture, we must play the towers about until they come right, as fearlessly as if they were chessmen instead of cathedrals). The dual arrangement of these towers would have been too easily seen, were it not for the little one which pretends to make a triad of the last group on the right, but is so faint as hardly to be discernible: it just takes off the attention from the artifice, helped in doing so by the mast at the head of the boat, which, however, has instantly its own duplicate put at the stern. Then there is the large boat near, and its echo beyond it. That echo is divided into two again, and each of those two smaller boats has two figures in it; while two figures are also sitting together on the great rudder that lies half in the water, and half aground. Then finally, the great mass of Ehrenbreitstein, which appears at first to have no answering form, has almost its *facsimile* in the bank on which the girl is sitting; this bank is as absolutely essential to the completion of the picture as any object in the whole series. All this is done to deepen the effect of repose.

Symmetry, or the balance of parts or masses in nearly equal opposition, is one of the conditions of treatment under the law of Repetition. For the opposition, in a symmetrical object, is of like things, reflecting each other: it is not the balance of contrary natures (like that of day and night), but of like natures or like forms; one side of a leaf being set like the reflection of the other in water.

In many sacred compositions, living symmetry, the balance of harmonious opposites, is one of the profoundest sources of their power: almost any works of the early painters, Angelico, Perugino, Giotto, &c., will furnish you with notable instances of it. The Madonna of Perugino in the National Gallery, with the angel Michael on one side and Raphael on the other, is as beautiful an example as you can have.

In landscape, the principle of balance is more or less carried out, in proportion to the wish of the painter to express disciplined calmness. In bad compositions, as in bad architecture, it is formal, a tree on one side answering a tree on the other; but in good compositions, as in graceful statues, it is always easy, and sometimes hardly traceable. In the Coblentz, however, you cannot have much difficulty in seeing how the boats on one side of the tower and the figures on the other are set in nearly equal balance; the tower, as a central mass, uniting both.

3. The Law of Continuity

Another important and pleasurable way of expressing unity is by giving some orderly succession to a number of objects more or less similar. And this succession is most interesting when it is connected with some gradual change in the aspect or character of the objects. Thus the succession of the pillars of a cathedral aisle is most interesting when they retire in perspective, becoming more and more obscure in distance: so the succession of mountain promontories one behind another, on the flanks of a valley; so the succession of clouds, fading farther and farther towards the horizon; each promontory and each cloud being of different shape, yet all evidently following in a calm and appointed order. If there be no change at all in the shape or size of the objects, there is no continuity; there is only repetition—monotony. It is the change in shape which suggests the idea of their being individually free, and able to escape, if they liked, from the law that rules them, and yet submitting to it.

I need not, I hope, point out to the reader the illustration of this law of continuance in the subject chosen for our general illustration.

It was simply that gradual succession of the retiring arches of the bridge which induced Turner to paint the subject at all; and it was this same principle which led him always to seize on subjects including long bridges wherever he could find them; but especially, observe, unequal bridges, having the highest arch at one side rather than at the centre.

We see that the Turnerian bridge in Fig. 2 is of the absolutely perfect type, and is still farther interesting by having its main arch crowned by a watch-tower. But as I want you to note especially what perhaps was not the case in the real bridge, but is entirely Turner's doing, you will find that though the arches diminish gradually, not one is *regularly* diminished—they are all of different shapes and sizes. This is indeed also part of the ideal of a bridge, because the lateral currents near the shore are of course irregular in size, and a simple builder would naturally vary his arches accordingly; and also, if the bottom was rocky, build his piers where the rocks came. But it is not as a part of bridge ideal, but as a necessity of all noble composition, that this irregularity is introduced by Turner. It at once raises the object thus treated from the lower or vulgar unity of rigid law to the greater unity of clouds, and waves, and trees, and human souls, each different, each obedient, and each in harmonious service.

4. The Law of Curvature

There is, however, another point to be noticed in this bridge of Turner's. Not only does it slope away unequally at its sides, but it slopes in a gradual though very subtle curve. And if you substitute a straight line for this curve (drawing one with a rule from the base of the tower on each side to the ends of the bridge, in Fig. 3, and effacing the curve), you will instantly see that the design has suffered grievously. You may ascertain, by experiment, that all beautiful objects whatsoever are thus terminated by delicately curved lines, except where the straight line is indispensable to their use or stability; and that when a complete system of straight lines, throughout

TURNER's *Coblentz Bridge.* FIG. 2.

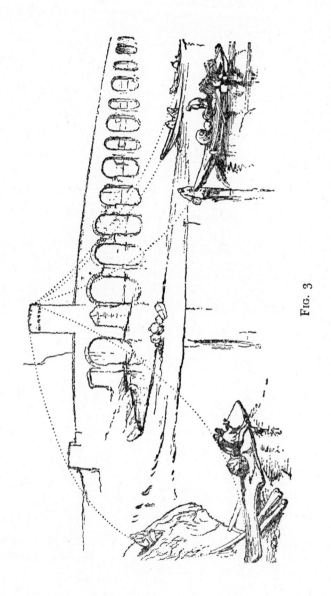

FIG. 3

the form, is necessary to that stability, as in crystals, the beauty, if any exists, is in colour and transparency, not in form. Cut out the shape of any crystal you like, in white wax or wood, and put it beside a white lily, and you will feel the force of the curvature in its purity, irrespective of added colour, or other interfering elements of beauty.

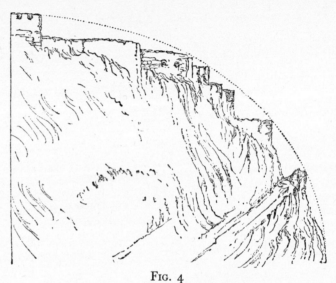

FIG. 4

Well, as curves are more beautiful than straight lines, it is necessary to a good composition that its continuities of object, mass, or colour should be, if possible, in curves, rather than straight lines or angular ones. Perhaps one of the simplest and prettiest examples of a graceful continuity of this kind is in the line traced at any moment by the corks of a net as it is being drawn: nearly every person is more or less attracted by the beauty of the dotted line. Now it is almost always possible, not only to secure such a continuity in the arrangement or boundaries of objects which, like these bridge arches or the corks of the net, are actually connected with each other, but— and this is a still more noble and interesting kind of continuity— among features which appear at first entirely separate. Thus the towers of Ehrenbreitstein, on the left, in Fig. 2, appear at first independent of each other; but when I give their profile, on a larger scale, Fig. 4, the reader may easily perceive that there is a subtle cadence and harmony among them. The reason of this is, that they are all bounded by one grand curve, traced by the dotted line; out of the seven towers, four precisely touch this curve, the others only falling back from it here and there to keep the eye from discovering it too easily.

And it is not only always *possible* to obtain continuities of this kind: it is, in drawing large forest or mountain forms, essential to truth. The towers of Ehrenbreitstein might or might not in reality fall into such a curve, but assuredly the basalt rock on which they stand did; for all mountain forms not cloven into absolute precipice, nor covered by straight slopes of shale, are more or less governed by these great curves, it being one of the aims of Nature in all her work to produce them.

Graceful curvature is distinguished from ungraceful by two characters: first, its moderation, that is to say, its close approach to straightness in some part of its course; and, secondly, by its variation, that is to say, its never remaining equal in degree at different parts of its course.

This variation is itself twofold in all good curves.

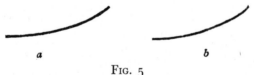

a b

Fig. 5

A. There is, first, a steady change through the whole line, from less to more curvature, or more to less, so that *no* part of the line is a segment of a circle, or can be drawn by compasses in any way whatever. Thus, in Fig. 5, *a* is a bad curve, because it is a part of a circle, and is therefore monotonous throughout; but *b* is a good curve, because it continually changes its direction as it proceeds.

The *first* difference between good and bad drawing of tree boughs consists in observance of this fact. Thus, when I put leaves on the line *b*, as in Fig. 6, you can immediately feel the springiness of character dependent on the changefulness of the curve. You may put leaves on the other line for yourself, but you will find you cannot

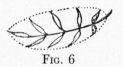

FIG. 6

make a right tree-spray of it. For *all* tree boughs, large or small, as well as all noble natural lines whatsoever, agree in this character; and it is a point of primal necessity that your eye should always seize and your hand trace it.

B. Not only does every good curve vary in general tendency, but it is modulated, as it proceeds, by myriads of subordinate curves, as in waves, clouds, and all other nobly formed masses. Thus another essential difference between good and bad drawing, or good and bad sculpture, depends on the quantity and refinement of minor curvatures carried, by good work, into the great lines. Strictly speaking, however, this is not variation in large curves, but composition of large curves out of small ones; it is an increase in the quantity of the beautiful element, *but not a change in its nature.*

5. *The Law of Radiation*

We have hitherto been concerned only with the binding of our various objects into beautiful lines or processions. The next point we have to consider is, how we may unite these lines or processions themselves, so as to make groups of *them.*

Now, there are two kinds of harmonies of lines. One in which, moving more or less side by side, they variously, but evidently with consent, retire from or approach each other, intersect or oppose each other: currents of melody in music, for different voices, thus approach and cross, fall and rise, in harmony; so the waves of the sea, as they approach the shore, flow into one another or cross, but with a great unity through all; and so various lines of composition often flow harmoniously through and across each other in a picture. But the most simple and perfect connexion of lines is by radiation; that is, by their all springing from one point, or closing towards it: and this harmony is often, in Nature almost always, united with the other; as the boughs of trees, though they intersect and play amongst each other irregularly, indicate by their general tendency their origin from one root. An essential part of the beauty of all vegetable form is in this radiation: it is seen most simply in a single flower or leaf, as in a convolvulus bell, or chestnut leaf; but more beautifully in the complicated arrangements of the large boughs and sprays. For a leaf is only a flat piece of radiation; but the tree throws its branches on all sides, and even in every profile view of it, which presents a radiation more or less correspondent to that of its leaves, it is more beautiful, because varied by the freedom of the separate branches.

This law of radiation, then, enforcing unison of action in arising from, or proceeding to, some given point, is perhaps, of all principles of composition, the most influential in producing the beauty of groups of form. Other laws make them forcible or interesting, but this generally is chief in rendering them beautiful. In the arrangement of masses in pictures, it is constantly obeyed by the great composers; but, like the law of principality, with careful concealment of its imperativeness, the point to which the lines of main curvature are directed being very often far away out of the picture. Sometimes, however, a system of curves will be employed definitely to exalt, by their concurrence, the value of some leading object, and then the law becomes traceable enough.

In the instance before us, the principal object being, as we have seen, the tower on the bridge, Turner has determined that his system of curvature should have its origin in the top of this tower. The diagram Fig. 3, compared with Fig. 2, will show how this is done. One curve joins the two towers, and is continued by the back of the figure sitting on the bank into the piece of bent timber. This is a limiting curve of great importance, and Turner has drawn a considerable part of it with the edge of the timber very carefully, and then led the eye up to the sitting girl by some white spots and indications of a ledge in the bank; then the passage to the tops of the towers cannot be missed.

The next curve is begun and drawn carefully for half an inch of its course by the rudder; it is then taken up by the basket and the heads of the figures, and leads accurately to the tower angle. The gunwales of both the boats begin the next two curves, which meet in the same point; and all are centralised by the long reflection which continues the vertical lines.

Subordinated to this first system of curves there is another, begun by the small crossing bar of wood inserted in the angle behind the rudder; continued by the bottom of the bank on which the figure sits, interrupted forcibly beyond it, but taken up again by the water-line leading to the bridge foot, and passing on in delicate shadows under the arches. This is a most important curve, indicating that the force and sweep of the river have indeed been in old times under the large arches; while the antiquity of the bridge is told us by the long tongue of land, either of carted rubbish, or washed down by some minor stream, which has interrupted this curve, and is now used as a landing place for the boats, and for embarkation of merchandise, of which some bales and bundles are laid in a heap, immediately beneath the great tower. A common composer would have put these bales to one side or the other, but Turner knows better; he uses them as a foundation for his tower, adding to its importance precisely as the sculptured base adorns a pillar; and he farther increases the aspect of its height by throwing the reflection of it far down in the nearer water. All the great composers have this same feeling about sustaining their vertical masses: you will constantly find Prout using the artifice most dexterously; and Veronese, Titian, and Tintoret continually put their principal figures at bases of pillars. Turner found out their secret very early, the most prominent instance of his composition on this principle being the drawing of Turin from the Superga, in Hakewell's Italy.

6. *The Law of Contrast*

Of course the character of everything is best manifested by Contrast. Rest can only be enjoyed after labour; sound, to be heard clearly, must rise out of silence; light is exhibited by darkness, darkness by light; and so on in all things. Now in art every colour has an opponent colour, which, if brought near it, will relieve it more completely than any other; so, also, every form and line may be made more striking to the eye by an opponent form or line near them; a curved line is set off by a straight one, a massy form by a slight one, and so on; and in all good work nearly double the value, which any given colour or form would have uncombined, is given to each by contrast.

In this case again, however, a too manifest use of the artifice vulgarises a picture. Great painters do not commonly, or very visibly, admit violent contrast. They introduce it by stealth, and with intermediate links of tender change; allowing, indeed, the opposition to tell upon the mind as a surprise, but not as a shock. Turner hardly ever, as far as I remember, allows a strong light to oppose a full dark, without some intervening tint. His suns never set behind dark mountains, without a film of cloud above the mountain's edge.

Thus in the rock of Ehrenbreitstein, Fig. 4, the main current of the lines being downwards, in a convex swell, they are suddenly stopped at the lowest tower by a counter series of beds, directed nearly straight across them. This adverse force sets off and relieves the great curvature, but it is reconciled to it by a series of radiating lines below, which at first sympathise with the oblique bar, then gradually get steeper, till they meet and join in the fall of the great curve. No passage, however intentionally monotonous, is ever introduced by a good artist without *some* slight counter current of this kind; so much, indeed, do the great composers feel the necessity of it, that they will even do things purposely ill or unsatisfactorily, in order to give greater value to their well-doing in other places. In a skilful poet's versification the so-called bad or inferior lines are not inferior because he could not do them better, but because he feels that if all were equally weighty, there would be no real sense of weight anywhere; if all were equally melodious, the melody itself would be fatiguing; and he purposely introduces the labouring or discordant verse, that the full ring may be felt in his main sentence, and the finished sweetness in his chosen rhythm. And continually in painting, inferior artists destroy their work by giving too much of all that they think is good, while the great painter gives just enough to be enjoyed, and passes to an opposite kind of enjoyment, or to an inferior state of enjoyment: he gives a passage of rich, involved, exquisitely wrought colour, then passes away into slight, and pale, and simple colour; he paints for a minute or two with intense decision, then suddenly becomes, as the spectator thinks, slovenly; but he is not slovenly: you could not have *taken* any more decision from him just then; you have had as much as is good for you: he paints over a great space of his picture forms of the most rounded and melting tenderness, and suddenly, as you think by a freak, gives you a bit as jagged and sharp as a leafless blackthorn. Perhaps the most exquisite piece of subtle contrast in the world of painting is the arrow point, laid sharp against the white side and among the flowing hair of Correggio's Antiope. It is quite singular how very little contrast will sometimes serve to make an entire group of forms interesting which would otherwise have been valueless.

You may not readily believe, at first, that all these laws are indeed involved in so trifling a piece of composition. But, as you study longer, you will discover that these laws, and many more, are obeyed by the powerful composers in every *touch*: that literally, there is never a dash of their pencil which is not carrying out appointed purposes of this kind in twenty various ways at once; and that there is as much difference, in way of intention and authority, between one of the great composers ruling his colours, and a common painter confused by them, as there is between a general directing the march of an army, and an old lady carried off her feet by a mob.

7. *The Law of Interchange*

Closely connected with the law of contrast is a law which enforces the unity of opposite things, by giving to each a portion of
the character of the other. If, for instance, you divide a shield into
two masses of colour, all the way down—suppose blue and white,
and put a bar, or figure of an animal, partly on one division, partly
on the other, you will find it pleasant to the eye if you make the
part of the animal blue which comes upon the white half, and white
which comes upon the blue half. This is done in heraldry, partly
for the sake of perfect intelligibility, but yet more for the sake of delight in interchange of colour, since, in all ornamentation whatever,
the practice is continual, in the ages of good design.

Sometimes this alternation is merely a reversal of contrasts; as
that, after red has been for some time on one side, and blue on
the other, red shall pass to blue's side and blue to red's. This kind of
alternation takes place simply in four-quartered shields; in more
subtle pieces of treatment, a little bit only of each colour is carried
into the other, and they are as it were dovetailed together. One of
the most curious facts which will impress itself upon you, when you
have drawn some time carefully from Nature in light and shade, is
the appearance of intentional artifice with which contrasts of this
alternate kind are produced by her; the artistry with which she will
darken a tree trunk as long as it comes against light sky, and throw
sunlight on it precisely at the spot where it comes against a dark
hill, and similarly treat all her masses of shade and colour, is so
great, that if you only follow her closely, everyone who looks at your
drawing with attention will think that you have been inventing the
most artificially and unnaturally delightful interchanges of shadow
that could possibly be devised by human wit.

You will find this law of interchange insisted upon at length by
Prout in his Lessons on Light and Shade: it seems, of all his principles of composition, to be the one he is most conscious of; many

others he obeys by instinct, but this he formally accepts and forcibly declares.

The typical purpose of the law of interchange is, of course, to teach us how opposite natures may be helped and strengthened by receiving each, as far as they can, some impress or reflection, or imparted power, from the other.

8. The Law of Consistency

It is to be remembered, in the next place, that while contrast exhibits the *characters* of things, it very often neutralises or paralyses their *power*. A number of white things may be shown to be clearly white by opposition of a black thing, but if we want the full power of their gathered light, the black thing may be seriously in our way. Thus, while contrast displays things, it is unity and sympathy which employ them, concentrating the power of several into a mass. And, not in art merely, but in all the affairs of life, the wisdom of man is continually called upon to reconcile these opposite methods of exhibiting, or using, the materials in his power. By change he gives them pleasantness, and by consistency value; by change he is refreshed, and by perseverance strengthened.

Hence many compositions address themselves to the spectator by aggregate force of colour or line, more than by contrasts of either; many noble pictures are painted almost exclusively in various tones of red, or grey, or gold, so as to be instantly striking by their breadth of flush, or glow, or tender coldness, these qualities being exhibited only by slight and subtle use of contrast. Similarly as to form; some compositions associate massive and rugged forms, others slight and graceful ones, each with few interruptions by lines of contrary character. And, in general, such compositions possess higher sublimity than those which are more mingled in their elements. They tell a special tale, and summon a definite state of feeling, while the grand compositions merely please the eye.

This unity or breadth of character generally attaches most to the works of the greatest men; their separate pictures have all separate aims. We have not, in each, gay colour set against sombre, and sharp forms against soft, and loud passages against low: but we have the bright picture, with its delicate sadness; the sombre picture, with its single ray of relief; the stern picture, with only one tender group of lines; the soft and calm picture, with only one rock angle at its flank; and so on. Hence the variety of their work, as well as its impressiveness. The principal bearing of this law, however, is on the separate masses or divisions of a picture: the character of the whole composition may be broken or various, if we please, but there must certainly be a tendency to consistent assemblage in its divisions. As an army may act on several points at once, but can only act effectually by having somewhere formed and regular masses, and not wholly by skirmishers; so a picture may be various in its tendencies, but must be somewhere united and coherent in its masses. Good composers are always associating their colours in great groups; binding their forms together by encompassing lines, and securing, by various dexterities of expedient, what they themselves call "breadth": that is to say, a large gathering of each kind of thing into one place; light being gathered to light, darkness to darkness, and colour to colour. If, however, this be done by introducing false lights or false colours, it is absurd and monstrous; the skill of a painter consists in obtaining breadth by rational arrangement of his objects, not by forced or wanton treatment of them. It is an easy matter to paint one thing all white, and another all black or brown; but not an easy matter to assemble all the circumstances which will naturally produce white in one place, and brown in another. Generally speaking, however, breadth will result in sufficient degree from fidelity of study: Nature is always broad; and if you paint her colours in true relations, you will paint them in majestic masses.

9. The Law of Harmony

This last law is not, strictly speaking, so much one of composition as of truth, but it must guide composition, and is properly, therefore, to be stated in this place.

Good drawing is, as we have seen, an *abstract* of natural facts; you cannot represent all that you would, but must continually be falling short, whether you will or no, of the force, or quantity, of Nature. Now, suppose that your means and time do not admit of your giving the depth of colour in the scene, and that you are obliged to paint it paler. If you paint all the colours proportionately paler, as if an equal quantity of tint had been washed away from each of them, you still obtain a harmonious, though not an equally forcible statement of natural fact. But if you take away the colours unequally, and leave some tints nearly as deep as they are in Nature, while others are much subdued, you have no longer a true statement. You cannot say to the observer, "Fancy all those colours a little deeper, and you will have the actual fact." However he adds in imagination, or takes away, something is sure to be still wrong. The picture is out of harmony.

I have now stated to you all the laws of composition which occur to me as capable of being illustrated or defined; but there are multitudes of others which, in the present state of my knowledge, I cannot define, and others which I never hope to define; and these the most important, and connected with the deepest powers of the art. The best part of every great work is always inexplicable: it is good because it is good; and innocently gracious, opening as the green of the earth, or falling as the dew of heaven.

All noble composition can be reached only by instinct; you cannot set yourself to arrange a subject; you may see it, and seize it, at all times, but never laboriously invent it. And your power of discerning what is best in expression, among natural subjects, depends wholly on the temper in which you keep your own mind; above all, on your living so much alone as to allow it to become acutely sensitive in its own stillness. Never force yourself to admire anything when you are not in the humour; but never force yourself away from what you feel to be lovely, in search of anything better: and gradually the deeper scenes of the natural world will unfold themselves to you in still increasing fulness of passionate power; and your difficulty will be no more to seek or to compose subjects, but only to choose one from among the multitude of melodious thoughts with which you will be haunted, thoughts which will of course be noble or original in proportion to your own depth of character and general power of mind; for it is not so much by the consideration you give to any single drawing, as by the previous discipline of your powers of thought, that the character of your composition will be determined. Simplicity of life will make you sensitive to the refinement and modesty of scenery, just as inordinate excitement and pomp of daily life will make you enjoy coarse colours and affected forms. Habits of patient comparison and accurate judgment will make your art precious, as they will make your actions wise; and every increase of noble enthusiasm in your living spirit will be measured by the reflection of its light upon the works of your hands.

INDEX

❦

SCRIPTURAL INDEX

❧

OLD TESTAMENT

NEW TESTAMENT

Where there is no vision the people perish
"Blindness is epidemic these days"
To have Eyes and see not